COOK
Instant!

*More than **115** quick & easy recipes for your electric pressure cooker*

Publications International, Ltd.

Pictured on the front cover: Jerk Pork and Sweet Potato Stew *(page 102)* and Balsamic Green Beans with Almonds *(page 220)*.

Pictured on the back cover *(clockwise from top left):* Cider Vinaigrette-Glazed Beets *(page 198)*, Easy Meatballs *(page 68)*, Classic Irish Oatmeal *(page 162)* and Savory Cod Stew *(page 156)*.

ISBN: 978-1-68022-983-7

Manufactured in China.

8 7 6 5 4 3 2 1

Microwave Cooking: Microwave ovens vary in wattage. Use the cooking times as guidelines and check for doneness before adding more time.

Note: The recipes in this book are for use in electric pressure cookers. While today's pressure cookers are built with safety features, you MUST follow the instructions which come with your pressure cooker. IF YOU DO NOT FOLLOW THE SAFETY INSTRUCTIONS CAREFULLY, INJURY OR DAMAGE MAY RESULT.

TABLE OF CONTENTS

PRESSURE COOKING 101

Welcome to the wonderful world of electric pressure cooking! Although the current craze makes it seem like a new invention, pressure cooking has actually been around for a few hundred years. Many people grew up hearing frightening stories of pressure cooker catastrophes—exploding pots and soup on the ceiling—but those days are long gone. There have been great changes and improvements in recent years to make modern pressure cookers completely safe, quiet and easy to use.

What exactly is a pressure cooker?

It's a simple concept: Liquid is heated in a heavy pot with a lid that locks and forms an airtight seal. Since the steam from the hot liquid is trapped inside and can't evaporate, the pressure increases and raises the boiling point of the contents in the pot, and these items cook faster at a higher temperature. In general, pressure cooking can reduce cooking time to about one third of the time used in conventional cooking methods—and typically the time spent on pressure cooking is hands off. (There's no peeking or stirring when food is being cooked under pressure.)

New and improved

Many of the electric pressure cookers on the market today are actually multi-cookers—versatile appliances that can be a pressure cooker, slow cooker, rice cooker, steamer and even a yogurt maker. The cooking programs you'll find on the different control panels are convenient shortcuts for some foods you may prepare regularly (rice, beans, stews, etc.) which use preset times and cooking levels. But you don't need any special settings to cook great food fast. In this book we'll explore the basics of pressure cooking with recipes that use customized cooking times and pressure levels. So you'll be able to cook a wide variety of delicious dishes no matter what buttons you have on your pressure cooker.

If you're accustomed to a stovetop pressure cooker, you'll need to make a few minor adjustments when using an electric one. Electric pressure cookers regulate heat automatically, so there's no worry about adjusting the heat on a burner to maintain pressure. Also, electric pressure cookers operate at less than the conventional pressure standard of 15 pounds per square inch (psi) used by stovetop pressure cookers. Most electric pressure cookers operate at 9 to 11 psi, which means that stovetop pressure cooker recipes can be adapted to electric models by adding a little more cooking time.

Pressure Cooker Components

Before beginning to cook, make sure you're familiar with the basic parts of your pressure cooker. There are some differences between brands, but they have many standard features in common. Always refer to your manual for more details and to answer questions about your specific model. (The parts are very similar but manufacturers often have different names for the same parts which can cause confusion.)

The **exterior pot** is where the electrical components are housed. It should never be immersed in water; to clean it, simply unplug the unit, wipe it with a damp cloth and dry it immediately.

The **inner pot** holds the food and fits snugly into the exterior pot. Typically made of stainless steel or aluminum with a nonstick coating, it is removable, and it can be washed by hand or some models can go in the dishwasher.

The **LED display** typically shows a time that indicates where the pressure cooker is in a particular function. For many models, the time counts down to zero from the number of minutes that were programmed. (The timing begins once the machine reaches pressure.)

The **steam release valve** (also called exhaust valve or pressure regulating valve) is on top of the lid and is used to seal the pot or release steam. To seal the pot, move the valve to the sealing or locked position; to release pressure, move the valve to the venting or open position. This valve can pop off to clean, and to make sure nothing is blocking it.

The **float valve** controls the amount of pressure inside the pressure cooker and indicates when pressure cooking is taking place—the valve rises once the contents of the pot reach working pressure; it drops down when all the pressure has been released after cooking.

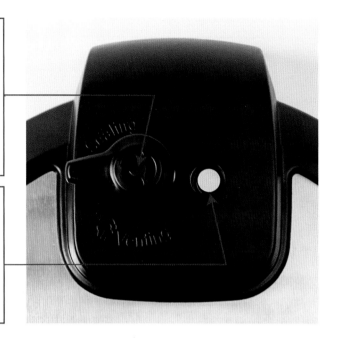

The **anti-block shield or case** is a small stainless steel cage found on the inside of the lid that prevents the pressure cooker from clogging. It can be removed for cleaning.

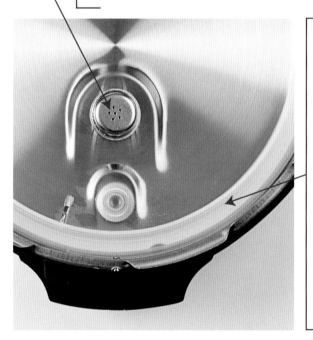

The **silicone sealing ring** (also called a gasket) underneath the lid helps create a tight seal to facilitate pressure cooking. The sealing ring has a tendency to absorb strong odors from cooking (particularly from acidic ingredients); washing it regularly with warm soapy water (or in the dishwasher if allowed) will help these odors dissipate, as will storing your pressure cooker with the lid ring side up. If you cook both sweet and savory dishes frequently, you may want to purchase an extra sealing ring (so the scent of curry or pot roast doesn't affect your rice pudding or crème brûlée). Make sure to inspect the ring before cooking—if it has any splits or cracks, it will not work properly and should be replaced.

Pressure Cooking Basics

Every recipe is slightly different, but most include these basic steps. Read through the entire recipe before beginning to cook so you'll know what ingredients to add and when to add them, which pressure level to use, the cooking time and the release method.

1. Sauté or brown: Many recipes call for sautéing vegetables or browning meat at the beginning of a recipe to add flavor. (Be sure to leave the lid off in this step.)

2. Add the ingredients as the recipe directs and secure the lid, making sure it is properly locked according to the instruction manual. Turn the pressure release valve to the sealing or locked position.

3. Choose the pressure level and set the cooking time. (The default setting is usually high pressure, which is what most recipes use.) Depending on your model, the pressure cooker may start automatically or you may need to press the Start button.

4. Once the pressure cooking is complete, use the pressure release method directed by the recipe. There are three types of releases:

Natural release: Let the pressure slowly release on its own, which can take anywhere from 5 to 25 minutes (but is typically in the 10- to 15-minute range). The release time will be shorter for a pot that is less full and longer for one that is more full. When the float valve lowers, the pressure is released and you can open the lid.

Quick release: Use a towel or pot holder to manually turn the pressure release valve to the venting or open position immediately after the cooking is complete. Be sure to get out of the way of the steam, and position the pressure cooker on your countertop so the steam doesn't get expelled straight into your cabinets (or in your face). It can take up to 2 minutes to fully release all the pressure.

A combination of natural and quick release: The recipe will instruct you to let the pressure release naturally for a certain amount of time (frequently for 10 minutes), and then do a quick release as directed.

Rules of Release

Releasing pressure can be a little confusing when you first start using your pressure cooker. There's no need to worry at all about safety—you won't be able to open the lid until all the pressure has been released. And you don't need to guess which release to use since the recipes will tell you. But there are some important things to know about releasing pressure, especially when you start cooking and experimenting with the pressure cooker on your own.

Natural release is best for meats (especially larger roasts and tough cuts), foods that generate a lot of foam, such as grains, dried beans and legumes, and foods that are primarily liquid, such as soups.

Quick release is best for foods with shorter cooking times, such as vegetables and eggs, and more delicate ingredients like fish and chicken breasts. It is also used when adding additional ingredients to the pot, as is the case with some stews and vegetable dishes, and to check whether a food is done.

A **combination release** is best when a full natural release is too slow but a quick release might cause food or foam to spray through the pressure release valve.

The release method does affect the cooking time—food continues to cook during a natural release due to the residual pressure and steam in the pot. So you may discover in some dishes that you prefer a shorter cooking time with a longer release time or vice versa. (Unfortunately the two times are not in direct proportion, so it can take some trial and error to figure out what works best.)

Control Panel Confusion

With so many different models of pressure cookers available, it's impossible to provide specific descriptions and directions for each one. To ensure safety and the best results when cooking, read the instructions in the user's manual before beginning.

The number of programs and their names vary from one pressure cooker to another, but there are a few key settings that are common to all models and are used in the recipes in this book.

Sauté or Brown

This function is used to cook or brown ingredients in the pot before cooking them under pressure. The default cooking temperature is medium on most pressure cookers (also called "normal" on some models). Some machines allow you to raise or lower the sauté temperature; others only offer one setting. And while many electric pressure cookers have a "Saute" button, others have a "Brown" button and some have both. If your model has both, the "Brown" function cooks at a higher temperature than "Saute." Sauté is also used to reduce and/or thicken the liquid left in the pot after cooking. Always leave the lid off when using the Sauté or Brown function.

Pressure Cooking

This control panel on your machine may have one button for high pressure and one for low pressure, or it may have a "Manual" button which allows you to choose which which pressure level you want to use. In either case, you'll need to enter the desired cooking time; some machines then start the program automatically and some require pressing a "Start" button to begin operation.

High pressure is used most often and is generally the default setting, as it allows the rapid cooking of meats, poultry, dense vegetables and frozen foods. Low pressure may be used for more delicate foods, including fish and some vegetables, and is frequently used in conjunction with a rack or steamer basket.

Cancel or Stop

This button is used to cancel a cooking program (such as when you are finished sautéing and are ready to start pressure cooking) or to turn off the pressure cooker. When the chosen time for pressure cooking is complete, some machines will automatically switch to the Keep Warm program; others require pressing the "Cancel" or "Stop" button.

Keep Warm

This function is used to keep cooked food warm until you're ready to serve, or to reheat food that has been allowed to cool.

Pressure Cooker Accessories

You don't need too many additional products when using a pressure cooker, but a few simple kitchen items are useful for certain recipes.

- A cooking rack or trivet comes with some models; this is used to elevate food above the cooking liquid. It can support ingredients (such as a turkey breast or cauliflower) or containers such as a baking dish or ramekins.

- Steamer baskets are also used to hold food, frequently vegetables. These can be made of metal, silicone or even bamboo—just be sure the size you have fits inside the pot. If your steamer basket doesn't have feet, you may need to place it on a rack or trivet to elevate it above the cooking liquid.

- Heatproof containers such as bowls, baking dishes and soufflé dishes are often used to cook desserts that contain a lot of liquid, such as custards and bread pudding, or anything that can't be placed in a steamer basket. They may be made of ceramic, metal, silicone or heatproof glass and are always used with a rack in the pressure cooker.

- Ramekins or custard cups serve the same purpose as larger containers but are useful in making single servings. They may also be made of ceramic, metal, silicone or heatproof glass, and they are used with a rack (stacked to fit in the pot).

Tips, Tricks, Dos and Don'ts

- Read the manual before beginning. There may be features you won't use, but it will eliminate some beginner's confusion and it can help you understand how the machine works—and see all its possibilities.

- Don't overfill the pot—the total amount of food and liquid should not exceed the maximum level marked on the inner pot. Generally it is best not to fill the pot more than two thirds full; when cooking foods that expand during cooking such as beans and grains, do not fill it more than half full.

- Make sure there is always some liquid in the pot before cooking because a minimum amount (usually 1 cup) is required to come up to pressure. (However, if the recipe contains a large amount of vegetables, you may be able to use a bit less since the vegetables will create their own liquid.)

- Always check that the pressure release valve is in the right position before you start pressure cooking. The food simply won't get cooked if the valve is not in the sealing or locked position because there will not be enough pressure in the pot.

- Never try to force the lid open after cooking—if the lid won't open, that means the pressure has not fully released. (As a safety feature, the lid remains locked until the float valve drops down.)

- Save the thickeners for after the pressure cooking is done. Pressure cooker recipes often end up with a lot of flavorful liquid left in the pot when cooking is complete; flour or cornstarch mixtures can thicken these liquids into delicious sauces. Use the Sauté or Brown function while incorporating the thickeners into the cooking liquid, and then cook and stir until the desired consistency is reached.

- Keep in mind that cooking times in some recipes may vary. We've included pressure cooking charts as a guide (pages 246—249), but these are approximate times, and numerous variables may cause your results to be different. For example, the freshness of dried beans affects their cooking time (older beans take longer to cook), as does what they are cooked with—hard water (water that is high in mineral content), acidic ingredients, sugar and salt levels can also affect cooking times. So be flexible and experiment with what works best for you—you can always check the doneness of your food and add more time.

- Set reasonable expectations, i.e., don't expect everything you cook in the pressure cooker to be ready in a few minutes. Even though it reduces many conventional cooking times dramatically, nothing is literally "instant"—it will always take time to get up to pressure, and then to release it. (These machines are fast but not magical!)

SOUPS

Curried Parsnip Soup

2 tablespoons butter or olive oil

1 medium yellow onion, chopped

2 stalks celery, diced

3 cloves garlic, minced

1 tablespoon salt

2 teaspoons curry powder

½ teaspoon grated fresh ginger

½ teaspoon black pepper

3 pounds parsnips, peeled and cut into 2-inch pieces

6 cups vegetable or chicken broth

Chopped fresh chives (optional)

1. Press Sauté; melt butter in pot. Add onion and celery; cook and stir 5 minutes or until onion is translucent. Add garlic, salt, curry powder, ginger and pepper; cook and stir 1 minute. Stir in parsnips and broth; mix well.

2. Secure lid and move pressure release valve to sealing or locked position. Cook at high pressure 10 minutes.

3. When cooking is complete, use natural release for 10 minutes, then release remaining pressure.

4. Use immersion blender to blend soup until smooth. (Or purée soup in batches in food processor or blender.) Garnish with chives.

Makes 6 to 8 servings

Minestrone Alla Milanese

¾ cup dried cannellini beans, soaked 8 hours or overnight

2 tablespoons olive oil

1 cup chopped carrots (½-inch pieces)

1 stalk celery, halved lengthwise and cut crosswise into ¼-inch slices

¾ cup chopped onion

2 cloves garlic, minced

1 container (32 ounces) vegetable broth

1 can (about 14 ounces) diced tomatoes

1 cup diced unpeeled red potato (about 1 large)

1 cup coarsely chopped green cabbage

1 small zucchini, halved lengthwise and cut crosswise into ¼-inch slices

¾ cup sliced fresh green beans

1½ teaspoons salt

½ teaspoon dried basil

¼ teaspoon dried rosemary

¼ teaspoon black pepper

1 bay leaf

Shredded Parmesan cheese (optional)

1. Drain and rinse dried beans. Press Sauté; heat oil in pot. Add carrots, celery and onion; cook and stir 5 minutes or until vegetables are softened. Add garlic; cook and stir 1 minute. Stir in broth, tomatoes, potato, cabbage, zucchini, green beans, salt, basil, rosemary, pepper and bay leaf; mix well.

2. Secure lid and move pressure release valve to sealing or locked position. Cook at high pressure 10 minutes.

3. When cooking is complete, use natural release for 15 minutes, then release remaining pressure. Remove and discard bay leaf. Garnish with cheese.

Makes 6 servings

Turkey Noodle Soup

1 tablespoon olive oil

1 onion, chopped

3 carrots, sliced

3 stalks celery, thinly sliced

2 cloves garlic, minced

1 teaspoon poultry seasoning

2 turkey drumsticks
(about 12 ounces each)

4 cups chicken broth

2 cups water

½ teaspoon salt

6 ounces uncooked egg noodles

⅓ cup chopped fresh Italian parsley

Black pepper

1. Press Sauté; heat oil in pot. Add onion; cook and stir 3 minutes or until softened. Add carrots, celery, garlic and poultry seasoning; cook and stir 3 minutes. Add drumsticks, broth, water and ½ teaspoon salt.

2. Secure lid and move pressure release valve to sealing or locked position. Cook at high pressure 35 minutes.

3. When cooking is complete, use natural release for 10 minutes, then release remaining pressure. Remove turkey to plate; set aside 10 minutes or until cool enough to handle.

4. Press Sauté; bring soup to a boil. Add noodles to pot; cook 8 minutes or until tender, stirring occasionally.

5. Meanwhile, remove and discard skin and bones from turkey; shred meat into bite-size pieces. Stir turkey and parsley into soup; cook until heated through. Season with additional salt and pepper.

Makes 6 servings

Potato Soup with Green Chiles and Cheese

1 tablespoon vegetable oil

1 medium onion, chopped

1 clove garlic, minced

1 tablespoon all-purpose flour

2 cups chopped unpeeled potatoes

2 cups chicken broth

½ teaspoon salt

½ teaspoon celery salt, divided

2 cups milk

1 can (4 ounces) diced green chiles, drained

¾ cup (3 ounces) shredded Monterey Jack cheese

¾ cup (3 ounces) shredded Colby or Cheddar cheese

1. Press Sauté; heat oil in pot. Add onion and garlic; cook and stir 3 minutes or until softened. Stir in flour until blended. Add potatoes, broth, salt and ¼ teaspoon celery salt; mix well.

2. Secure lid and move pressure release valve to sealing or locked position. Cook at high pressure 4 minutes.

3. When cooking is complete, press Cancel or Stop and use quick release.

4. Press Sauté; adjust heat to low. Add milk, chiles and remaining ¼ teaspoon celery salt; cook 5 minutes, stirring occasionally. Add Monterey Jack and Colby cheeses; cook and stir just until cheeses are melted. (Do not boil.)

Makes 4 to 6 servings

Easy Corn Chowder

6 slices bacon, chopped

1 medium onion, diced

1 stalk celery, sliced

1 red bell pepper, diced

1 package (16 ounces) frozen corn, thawed

3 small potatoes, peeled and cut into ½-inch pieces (about 2 cups)

½ teaspoon ground coriander

3 cups chicken broth

½ teaspoon salt

½ teaspoon black pepper

¼ teaspoon ground red pepper

½ cup whipping cream

1. Press Sauté; cook bacon in pot until crisp. Remove to paper towel-lined plate. Drain off all but 1 tablespoon drippings.

2. Add onion, celery and bell pepper to pot; cook and stir 3 minutes or until vegetables are softened. Add corn, potatoes and coriander; cook and stir 1 minute. Stir in broth, salt, black pepper and ground red pepper; mix well.

3. Secure lid and move pressure release valve to sealing or locked position. Cook at high pressure 4 minutes.

4. When cooking is complete, use natural release for 10 minutes, then release remaining pressure.

5. Press Sauté; cook 2 to 3 minutes or until soup is thickened, partially mashing potatoes. Stir in cream; cook until heated through. Top with bacon.

Makes 4 servings

Chicken Tortilla Soup

2 cans (about 14 ounces each) diced tomatoes

1½ pounds boneless skinless chicken thighs

1 onion, diced

1 can (4 ounces) diced green chiles

½ cup chicken broth

2 cloves garlic, minced

1 teaspoon ground cumin

1 teaspoon salt

¼ teaspoon black pepper

4 corn tortillas, cut into ¼-inch strips

2 tablespoons chopped fresh cilantro

½ cup (2 ounces) shredded Monterey Jack cheese

1 avocado, diced and tossed with lime juice

Lime wedges

1. Combine tomatoes, chicken, chiles, broth, onion, garlic, cumin, salt and pepper in pot; mix well.

2. Secure lid and move pressure release valve to sealing or locked position. Cook at high pressure 9 minutes.

3. When cooking is complete, use natural release for 10 minutes, then release remaining pressure.

4. Remove chicken to plate; shred into bite-size pieces when cool enough to handle. Stir into soup.

5. Press Sauté; add tortillas and cilantro to soup. Cook and stir 2 minutes or until heated through. Top with cheese, avocado and squeeze of lime juice. Serve immediately.*

Soup can be made ahead through step 3. When ready to serve, heat soup to a simmer; add tortilla strips and cilantro and cook until heated through.

Makes 4 to 6 servings

Middle Eastern Lentil Soup

2 tablespoons olive oil

1 small onion, chopped

1 medium red bell pepper, chopped

1 teaspoon whole fennel seeds

½ teaspoon ground cumin

¼ teaspoon ground red pepper

4 cups water

1 cup dried lentils, rinsed and sorted

1½ teaspoons salt

1 tablespoon lemon juice

½ cup plain yogurt

Chopped fresh parsley

1. Press Sauté; heat oil in pot. Add onion and bell pepper; cook and stir 3 minutes or until vegetables are softened. Add fennel seeds, cumin and ground red pepper; cook and stir 1 minute. Stir in water, lentils and salt; mix well.

2. Secure lid and move pressure release valve to sealing or locked position. Cook at high pressure 17 minutes.

3. When cooking is complete, use natural release for 10 minutes, then release remaining pressure.

4. Stir in lemon juice. Top soup with yogurt; sprinkle with parsley.

Makes 4 servings

Serving Suggestion: Serve with homemade pita chips. Cut 4 pita bread rounds into 6 wedges each. Spread pita wedges on large baking sheet. Brush with 1 tablespoon olive oil; sprinkle with 1 teaspoon coarse salt. Bake at 350°F 15 minutes or until lightly browned and crisp.

Bean and Pasta Soup

1¼ cups dried navy beans, soaked 8 hours or overnight

3 slices bacon, finely chopped

1 onion, chopped

1 stalk celery, chopped

1 carrot, chopped

2 cloves garlic, minced

4 cups water

1 smoked ham hock (8 to 12 ounces)

½ teaspoon salt

½ teaspoon dried thyme

½ teaspoon dried marjoram

¼ teaspoon black pepper

¾ cup uncooked small pasta shells

2 tablespoons chopped fresh parsley

½ to 1 cup chicken broth (optional)

Grated Parmesan cheese (optional)

1. Drain and rinse beans. Press Sauté; cook bacon in pot until crisp. Add onion, celery and carrot; cook and stir 5 minutes or until golden brown, scraping up browned bits from bottom of pot. Add garlic; cook and stir 30 seconds. Add beans, water, ham hock, salt, thyme, marjoram and pepper; mix well.

2. Secure lid and move pressure release valve to sealing or locked position. Cook at high pressure 16 minutes.

3. When cooking is complete, use natural release for 10 minutes, then release remaining pressure.

4. Remove ham hock to plate. Use immersion blender to partially blend soup, leaving soup chunky. (Or transfer half of soup to food processor or blender; process until smooth and return puréed soup to pot.)

5. Press Sauté; bring soup to a boil. Stir in pasta. Adjust heat to low; cook about 10 minutes or until pasta is tender, stirring occasionally.

6. Meanwhile, remove meat from ham hock; chop into bite-size pieces. Stir meat and parsley into soup. Thin soup with broth, if necessary. Serve with cheese, if desired.

Makes 4 servings

Cauliflower Bisque

1 head cauliflower (about 1½ pounds), broken into florets

1 large baking potato (about 1 pound), peeled and cut into 1-inch pieces

2 cans (about 14 ounces each) vegetable or chicken broth

1 cup chopped onion

½ teaspoon dried thyme

1 clove garlic, minced

1 teaspoon salt

⅛ teaspoon ground red pepper (optional)

⅛ teaspoon black pepper

1 can (5 ounces) evaporated milk

2 tablespoons butter

1 cup (4 ounces) shredded Cheddar cheese

¼ cup finely chopped fresh parsley

¼ cup finely chopped green onions

1. Combine cauliflower, potato, broth, onion, garlic, salt, thyme, red pepper, if desired, and black pepper in pot; mix well.

2. Secure lid and move pressure release valve to sealing or locked position. Cook at high pressure 5 minutes.

3. When cooking is complete, use natural release for 10 minutes, then release remaining pressure.

4. Use immersion blender to blend soup in pot until smooth (or purée soup in batches in food processor or blender). Stir in evaporated milk and butter until blended. Serve with cheese, parsley and green onions.

Makes 6 servings

Split Pea Soup

8 slices bacon, chopped

1 onion, chopped

2 carrots, chopped

1 stalk celery, chopped

1 clove garlic, minced

½ teaspoon dried thyme

1 container (32 ounces) chicken broth

2 cups water

1 package (16 ounces) dried split peas, rinsed and sorted

¾ teaspoon salt

½ teaspoon black pepper

1 bay leaf

1. Press Sauté; cook and stir bacon in pot until crisp. Remove to paper towel-lined plate. Drain off all but 1 tablespoon drippings.

2. Add onion, carrots and celery to pot; cook and stir 5 minutes or until vegetables are softened. Add garlic and thyme; cook and stir 1 minute. Stir in broth and water, scraping up browned bits from bottom of pot. Add split peas, half of bacon, salt, pepper and bay leaf; mix well.

3. Secure lid and move pressure release valve to sealing or locked position. Cook at high pressure 8 minutes.

4. When cooking is complete, use natural release for 10 minutes, then release remaining pressure. Stir soup; remove and discard bay leaf. Garnish with remaining bacon.

Makes 4 to 6 servings

Note: The soup may appear thin immediately after cooking, but it will thicken upon standing. If prepared in advance and refrigerated, thin the soup with water when reheating it until it reaches the desired consistency.

Spicy Squash and Chicken Soup

1 tablespoon vegetable oil

1 small onion, finely chopped

1 stalk celery, finely chopped

2 cups chicken broth

2 cups cubed butternut squash (1-inch pieces)

1 can (about 14 ounces) diced tomatoes with chiles

8 ounces boneless skinless chicken thighs, cut into ½-inch pieces

½ teaspoon salt

½ teaspoon ground ginger

⅛ teaspoon ground cumin

⅛ teaspoon black pepper

2 teaspoons lime juice

½ to 1 teaspoon hot pepper sauce

Fresh cilantro or parsley sprigs (optional)

1. Press Sauté; heat oil in pot. Add onion and celery; cook and stir 5 minutes or until vegetables are softened. Add broth, squash, tomatoes, chicken, salt, ginger, cumin and black pepper; mix well.

2. Secure lid and move pressure release valve to sealing or locked position. Cook at high pressure 5 minutes.

3. When cooking is complete, use natural release for 10 minutes, then release remaining pressure.

4. Stir in lime juice and hot pepper sauce; garnish with cilantro.

Makes 4 servings

Hearty White Bean Soup

1½ cups dried navy beans, soaked 8 hours or overnight

2 tablespoons olive oil

1 cup chopped onion

1 cup chopped carrots

1 cup chopped red or green bell pepper

½ cup chopped celery

2 cloves garlic, minced

1 tablespoon chopped fresh oregano *or* 1 teaspoon dried oregano

1½ teaspoons chopped fresh thyme *or* ¾ teaspoon dried thyme

½ teaspoon ground cumin

4 cups vegetable or chicken broth

3 cups water

2 teaspoons salt

¼ teaspoon black pepper

1. Drain and rinse beans. Press Sauté; heat oil in pot. Add onion; cook and stir 3 minutes or until softened. Add carrots, bell pepper and celery; cook and stir 3 minutes. Add garlic, oregano, thyme and cumin; cook and stir 1 minute. Stir in beans, broth, water, salt and black pepper; mix well.

2. Secure lid and move pressure release valve to sealing or locked position. Cook at high pressure 15 minutes.

3. When cooking is complete, use natural release.

Makes 6 servings

Potato and Leek Soup

8 ounces bacon, chopped

1 leek, diced

1 onion, chopped

2 carrots, diced

4 cups chicken broth

3 potatoes, peeled and diced

1½ cups chopped cabbage

1½ teaspoons salt

½ teaspoon caraway seeds

½ teaspoon black pepper

1 bay leaf

½ cup sour cream

Chopped fresh parsley (optional)

1. Press Sauté; cook bacon in pot until crisp. Remove to paper towel-lined plate. Drain off all but 2 tablespoons drippings.

2. Add leek, onion and carrots to pot; cook and stir about 4 minutes or until vegetables are softened. Stir in broth, scraping up browned bits from bottom of pot. Stir in potatoes, cabbage, salt, caraway seeds, pepper and bay leaf; mix well.

3. Secure lid and move pressure release valve to sealing or locked position. Cook at high pressure 4 minutes.

4. When cooking is complete, use natural release for 10 minutes, then release remaining pressure. Remove and discard bay leaf.

5. Whisk ½ cup hot soup into sour cream in small bowl until blended. Add sour cream mixture and bacon to soup; mix well. Garnish with parsley.

Makes 6 servings

Creamy Carrot Soup

1 tablespoon butter

½ cup chopped onion

1 tablespoon chopped fresh ginger

1 pound baby carrots or regular carrots, cut into 2-inch pieces

½ teaspoon salt

¼ teaspoon black pepper

3 cups vegetable broth

¼ cup whipping cream

2 tablespoons orange juice

Pinch ground nutmeg

4 tablespoons sour cream (optional)

Fresh parsley sprigs (optional)

1. Press Sauté; melt butter in pot. Add onion and ginger; cook and stir 1 minute or until ginger is fragrant. Add carrots, salt and pepper; cook and stir 2 minutes. Stir in broth.

2. Secure lid and move pressure release valve to sealing or locked position. Cook at high pressure 6 minutes.

3. When cooking is complete, use natural release for 10 minutes, then release remaining pressure.

4. Use immersion blender to blend soup until smooth. (Or purée soup in batches in food processor or blender.)

5. Press Sauté; adjust heat to low. Add cream, orange juice and nutmeg; cook until heated through, stirring frequently. (Do not boil.) Garnish with sour cream and parsley.

Makes 4 servings

Mushroom Barley Soup

2 tablespoons olive oil

1 onion, chopped

2 carrots, chopped

2 stalks celery, chopped

3 cloves garlic, minced

1 teaspoon salt

½ teaspoon dried thyme

½ teaspoon black pepper

5 cups vegetable or chicken broth

1 package (16 ounces) sliced fresh mushrooms

½ cup uncooked pearl barley

½ ounce dried porcini or shiitake mushrooms

1. Press Sauté; heat oil in pot. Add onion, carrots and celery; cook and stir 4 minutes or until vegetables are softened. Add garlic, salt, thyme and pepper; cook and stir 1 minute. Stir in broth, sliced mushrooms, barley and dried mushrooms; mix well.

2. Secure lid and move pressure release valve to sealing or locked position. Cook at high pressure 22 minutes.

3. When cooking is complete, use natural release for 10 minutes, then release remaining pressure.

Makes 6 to 8 servings

Vegetable Bean Soup

1 cup dried Great Northern beans, soaked 8 hours or overnight

1 tablespoon olive oil

1 cup chopped onion

¾ cup chopped carrots

3 cloves garlic, minced

4 cups coarsely chopped green cabbage

4 cups coarsely chopped unpeeled red potatoes (about 4 medium)

1 teaspoon dried rosemary

4 cups vegetable broth

1 can (about 14 ounces) diced tomatoes

1½ teaspoons salt

½ teaspoon black pepper

Grated Parmesan cheese (optional)

1. Drain and rinse beans. Press Sauté; heat oil in pot. Add onion and carrots; cook and stir 3 minutes or until vegetables are softened. Add garlic; cook and stir 30 seconds. Add cabbage, potatoes and rosemary; cook and stir 1 minute. Stir in beans, broth, tomatoes, salt and pepper; mix well.

2. Secure lid and move pressure release valve to sealing or locked position. Cook at high pressure 7 minutes.

3. When cooking is complete, use natural release for 10 minutes, then release remaining pressure. Serve with cheese, if desired.

Makes 6 to 8 servings

Beef Stock

2 pounds meaty beef bones

2½ tablespoons tomato paste

1 large onion, top and roots removed, brown outer skin intact, cut into wedges

1 large carrot, cut into large pieces

2 stalks celery, cut into large pieces

8 cups water, divided

4 sprigs fresh parsley

1 bay leaf

½ teaspoon salt

3 whole black peppercorns

1. Preheat oven to 450°F. Spread bones in roasting pan; roast 30 minutes or until browned, turning once. Spread tomato paste over bones; top with onion, carrot and celery. Return pan to oven; roast bones and vegetables 30 minutes. Remove bones and vegetables to pot.

2. Skim excess fat from roasting pan and discard. Pour 1 cup water into roasting pan; cook and stir 2 minutes over medium-high heat or until liquid is reduced by half, scraping up browned bits from bottom of pan. Pour into pot. Add remaining 7 cups water, parsley, bay leaf, salt and peppercorns; mix well.

3. Secure lid and move pressure release valve to sealing or locked position. Cook at high pressure 90 minutes.

4. When cooking is complete, use natural release.

5. Strain stock into large bowl through fine-mesh strainer or colander lined with several layers of damp cheesecloth; discard solids. To remove fat, cover and refrigerate stock overnight; fat will rise to the top and can be easily skimmed off the next day. Stock can be refrigerated up to 3 days or frozen up to 3 months.

Makes about 7 cups

Chicken Stock

8 cups water

1 onion, cut into quarters

1 clove garlic, cut in half

1 bay leaf

3 sprigs fresh parsley

½ teaspoon salt

3 whole black peppercorns

2 pounds bone-in chicken pieces (wings, backs and/or leg quarters, cut up)

1. Combine water, onion, garlic, bay leaf, parsley, salt and peppercorns in pot; mix well. Add chicken to pot.

2. Secure lid and move pressure release valve to sealing or locked position. Cook at high pressure 60 minutes.

3. When cooking is complete, use natural release.

4. Strain stock into large bowl through fine-mesh strainer or colander lined with several layers of damp cheesecloth. If there is meat remaining after cooking, set aside for soup or other recipes calling for cooked chicken; discard remaining solids. To remove fat, cover and refrigerate stock overnight; fat will rise to the top and can be easily skimmed off the next day. Stock can be refrigerated up to 3 days or frozen up to 3 months.

Makes about 8 cups

Vegetable Stock

8 cups water

2 large onions, cut into wedges

6 medium carrots, cut into 2-inch pieces

3 stalks celery, cut into 2-inch pieces

6 sprigs fresh parsley

2 cloves garlic, crushed

2 bay leaves

1 teaspoon salt

4 whole black peppercorns

1. Combine water, onions, carrots, celery, parsley, garlic, bay leaves, salt and peppercorns in pot; mix well.

2. Secure lid and move pressure release valve to sealing or locked position. Cook at high pressure 30 minutes.

3. When cooking is complete, use natural release.

4. Strain stock into large bowl through fine-mesh strainer or colander lined with several layers of damp cheesecloth; discard solids. Stock can be refrigerated up to 3 days or frozen up to 3 months.

Makes about 8 cups

BEEF

Sweet and Savory Brisket

1 teaspoon salt, divided

½ teaspoon black pepper

1 small beef brisket (2½ to 3 pounds), trimmed

1 large onion, thinly sliced

½ cup beef or chicken broth

⅓ cup chili sauce

1 tablespoon packed brown sugar

½ teaspoon dried thyme

¼ teaspoon ground cinnamon

2 large sweet potatoes, peeled and cut into 1-inch pieces

1 cup pitted prunes

¼ cup water

2 tablespoons cornstarch

1. Rub ½ teaspoon salt and pepper into all sides of beef. Place beef in pot; top with onion. Combine broth, chili sauce, brown sugar, thyme, cinnamon and remaining ½ teaspoon salt in small bowl; mix well. Pour over beef and onion.

2. Secure lid and move pressure release valve to sealing or locked position. Cook at high pressure 70 minutes.

3. When cooking is complete, use natural release for 10 minutes, then release remaining pressure. Remove beef to cutting board; cover loosely to keep warm.

4. Add sweet potatoes and prunes to pot. Secure lid and move pressure release valve to sealing or locked position. Cook at high pressure 3 minutes. When cooking is complete, press Cancel or Stop and use quick release. Remove vegetables to medium bowl with slotted spoon.

5. Stir water into cornstarch in small bowl until smooth. Press Sauté. Add cornstarch mixture to cooking liquid in pot; cook and stir 1 to 2 minutes or until sauce thickens.

6. Cut brisket into thin slices across the grain. Serve with sweet potato mixture and sauce.

Makes 4 servings

Braised Chipotle Beef

3 pounds boneless beef chuck roast, cut into 1-inch pieces

2 teaspoons salt, divided

¾ teaspoon black pepper, divided

3 tablespoons vegetable oil, divided

1 large onion, cut into 1-inch pieces

2 red bell peppers, cut into 1½-inch pieces

3 tablespoons tomato paste

1 tablespoon minced garlic

1 tablespoon chipotle chili powder*

1 tablespoon paprika

1 tablespoon ground cumin

1 teaspoon dried oregano

¼ cup water

1 can (about 14 ounces) diced tomatoes

Hot cooked rice or tortillas (optional)

*Or substitute regular chili powder.

1. Pat beef dry with paper towels; season with ½ teaspoon salt and ¼ teaspoon black pepper.

2. Press Sauté; heat 2 tablespoons oil in pot. Add beef in batches; cook about 4 minutes or until browned on all sides. Remove to plate.

3. Add remaining 1 tablespoon oil to pot. Add onion; cook and stir 3 minutes or until softened. Add bell peppers; cook and stir 2 minutes. Add tomato paste, garlic, chili powder, paprika, cumin, oregano, remaining 1½ teaspoons salt and ½ teaspoon black pepper; cook and stir 1 minute. Stir in water, scraping up browned bits from bottom of pot. Return beef to pot with tomatoes; mix well.

4. Secure lid and move pressure release valve to sealing or locked position. Cook at high pressure 30 minutes.

5. When cooking is complete, use natural release for 10 minutes, then release remaining pressure. Serve with rice or tortillas, if desired.

Makes 4 to 6 servings

Serving Suggestions: Add rice and/or beans to the Braised Chipotle Beef and use it as a filling for tacos or burritos. Or serve over mashed potatoes.

Pressure Cooker Meat Loaf

1 tablespoon olive oil

1 small onion, chopped

½ red bell pepper, chopped

3 cloves garlic, minced

1 teaspoon dried oregano

1½ cups water

2 pounds ground meat loaf mix or 1 pound *each* ground beef and ground pork

1 egg

3 tablespoons tomato paste

1 teaspoon salt

½ teaspoon black pepper

1. Press Sauté; heat oil in pot. Add onion, bell pepper, garlic and oregano; cook and stir 3 minutes or until vegetables are softened. Remove to large bowl; let cool 5 minutes. Wipe out pot with paper towels; add water and rack to pot.

2. Add meat, egg, tomato paste, salt and black pepper to onion mixture; mix well. Tear off 18×12-inch piece of foil; fold in half crosswise to create 12×9-inch rectangle. Shape meat mixture into 7×5-inch oval on foil; bring up sides of foil to create pan, leaving top of meat loaf uncovered. Place foil with meat loaf on rack in pot.

3. Secure lid and move pressure release valve to sealing or locked position. Cook at high pressure 37 minutes.

4. When cooking is complete, press Cancel or Stop and use quick release. Remove meat loaf to cutting board; let stand 10 minutes before slicing.

Makes 6 servings

Espresso-Laced Pot Roast

1 tablespoon packed brown sugar

1 tablespoon espresso powder

1½ teaspoons salt, divided

1 teaspoon black pepper, divided

1 boneless beef chuck pot roast (2 to 2½ pounds)

1½ tablespoons vegetable oil

1 large onion, chopped

1 cup beef broth

½ teaspoon dried thyme

2 bay leaves

6 to 8 red potatoes (about 2 pounds), peeled and cut into 1-inch pieces

1 pound carrots, cut into 1-inch pieces

3 tablespoons water

2 tablespoons all-purpose flour

Chopped fresh parsley (optional)

1. Combine brown sugar, espresso, ½ teaspoon salt and ½ teaspoon pepper in small bowl; mix well. Rub espresso mixture into all sides of beef.

2. Press Sauté; heat oil in pot. Add beef; cook about 6 minutes or until browned on all sides. Remove to plate. Add onion to pot; cook and stir 3 minutes or until softened. Add broth, thyme, bay leaves, remaining 1 teaspoon salt and ½ teaspoon pepper; cook and stir 2 minutes, scraping up browned bits from bottom of pot. Return beef to pot.

3. Secure lid and move pressure release valve to sealing or locked position. Cook at high pressure 60 minutes.

4. When cooking is complete, press Cancel or Stop and use quick release. Add potatoes and carrots to pot, pressing vegetables into cooking liquid. Secure lid and move pressure release valve to sealing or locked position. Cook at high pressure 4 minutes.

5. When cooking is complete, press Cancel or Stop and use quick release. Remove beef and vegetables to platter; cover loosely to keep warm. Remove and discard bay leaves.

6. Stir water into flour in small bowl until smooth. Press Sauté. Add flour mixture to cooking liquid in pot; cook about 5 minutes or until sauce is reduced and thickened, stirring frequently. Serve sauce with beef and vegetables; garnish with parsley.

Makes 4 to 6 servings

Bacon and Stout Short Ribs

6 slices thick-cut bacon, chopped

4 pounds bone-in beef short ribs, trimmed and cut into 3-inch pieces

1 teaspoon salt, divided

½ teaspoon black pepper

1 large onion, cut in half and thinly sliced

1 tablespoon tomato paste

1 bottle or can (12 ounces) stout, dark beer or ale

2 tablespoons spicy brown mustard

1 bay leaf

3 tablespoons cold water

2 tablespoons all-purpose flour

2 tablespoons finely chopped fresh parsley

Mashed potatoes or hot cooked egg noodles (optional)

1. Press Sauté; cook bacon in pot until crisp. Remove to paper towel-lined plate. Drain off all but 1 tablespoon drippings.

2. Season short ribs with ½ teaspoon salt and pepper. Add short ribs to pot, a few at a time; cook until browned on all sides. Remove to plate. Drain off all but 1 tablespoon fat.

3. Add onion to pot; cook and stir 5 minutes or until golden brown. Add tomato paste; cook and stir 1 minute. Add stout, mustard, bay leaf and remaining ½ teaspoon salt; cook and stir 1 minute, scraping up browned bits from bottom of pot. Return bacon and short ribs to pot.

4. Secure lid and move pressure release valve to sealing or locked position. Cook at high pressure 45 minutes.

5. When cooking is complete, use natural release for 10 minutes, then release remaining pressure. Remove short ribs to plate; cover loosely to keep warm. Remove and discard bay leaf.

6. Skim excess fat from surface of sauce. Stir water into flour in small bowl until smooth. Press Sauté; add flour mixture to cooking liquid in pot, stirring constantly. Cook and stir sauce about 5 minutes or until thickened. Stir in parsley. Serve sauce with short ribs and mashed potatoes, if desired.

Makes 4 to 6 servings

Tex-Mex Chili

4 slices bacon, chopped

⅓ cup all-purpose flour

1½ teaspoons salt, divided

¼ teaspoon black pepper

2 pounds boneless beef top round or chuck shoulder steak, cut into ½-inch pieces

1 medium onion, chopped, plus additional for garnish

2 cloves garlic, minced

1¼ cups water

¼ cup chili powder

1 teaspoon dried oregano

1 teaspoon ground cumin

½ to 1 teaspoon ground red pepper

½ teaspoon hot pepper sauce

1. Press Sauté; cook bacon in pot until crisp. Remove to paper towel-lined plate.

2. Combine flour, ½ teaspoon salt and black pepper in large resealable food storage bag. Add beef; toss to coat; Shake off any excess flour mixture. Add beef to bacon drippings in two batches; cook until browned on all sides. Remove to plate.

3. Add onion to pot; cook and stir 3 minutes or until softened. Add garlic; cook and stir 1 minute. Return beef and bacon to pot. Add water, chili powder, remaining 1 teaspoon salt, oregano, cumin, red pepper and hot pepper sauce; cook and stir minutes, scraping up browned bits from bottom of pot.

4. Secure lid and move pressure release valve to sealing or locked position. Cook at high pressure 20 minutes.

5. When cooking is complete, use natural release for 10 minutes, then release remaining pressure. Serve with additional chopped onion, if desired.

Makes 4 to 6 servings

Tip: Texas chili doesn't contain any beans. But if you want to stretch this recipe and dilute some of the spiciness—and you don't live in Texas!—you can add canned pinto beans to the chili after the pressure has been released. Press Sauté and cook until the beans are heated through.

Shortcut Bolognese

1 tablespoon olive oil

1 pound ground beef

1 medium onion, chopped

½ small carrot, finely chopped

½ stalk celery, finely chopped

3 tablespoons tomato paste

1 cup dry white wine

½ cup milk

⅛ teaspoon ground nutmeg

1 can (about 14 ounces) whole tomatoes, undrained, coarsely chopped

½ cup beef broth

1 teaspoon salt

1 teaspoon dried basil

½ teaspoon dried thyme

⅛ teaspoon black pepper

1 bay leaf

Hot cooked spaghetti

Grated Parmesan cheese (optional)

1. Press Sauté; heat oil in pot. Add beef; cook about 8 minutes or until all liquid evaporates, stirring to break up meat. Drain fat.

2. Add onion, carrot and celery to pot; cook and stir 4 minutes. Add tomato paste; cook and stir 2 minutes. Add wine; cook about 5 minutes or until wine has almost evaporated. Add milk and nutmeg; cook and stir 3 to 4 minutes or until milk has almost evaporated. Stir in tomatoes with liquid, broth, salt, basil, thyme, pepper and bay leaf; mix well.

3. Secure lid and move pressure release valve to sealing or locked position. Cook at high pressure 18 minutes.

4. When cooking is complete, press Cancel or Stop and use quick release. Remove and discard bay leaf. Serve sauce with spaghetti; top with cheese, if desired.

Makes 4 servings

Corned Beef and Cabbage

1 corned beef brisket
(3 to 4 pounds) with
seasoning packet

2 cups water

1 head cabbage (1½ pounds),
cut into 6 wedges

1 package (16 ounces)
baby carrots

1. Place corned beef in pot, fat side up; sprinkle with seasoning. Pour water into pot.

2. Secure lid and move pressure release valve to sealing or locked position. Cook at high pressure 90 minutes.

3. When cooking is complete, use natural release for 10 minutes, then release remaining pressure. Remove beef to cutting board; cover loosely to keep warm.

4. Add cabbage and carrots to pot. Secure lid and move pressure release valve to sealing or locked position. Cook at high pressure 4 minutes.

5. When cooking is complete, press Cancel or Stop and use quick release. Slice beef; serve with vegetables.

Makes 3 to 4 servings

Traditional Goulash

⅓ cup all-purpose flour

2½ teaspoons salt, divided

1 teaspoon black pepper

2 pounds boneless beef chuck shoulder, cut into bite-size pieces

2 to 3 tablespoons vegetable oil, divided

2 shallots *or* 1 medium onion, finely chopped

3 cloves garlic, minced

1 can (28 ounces) diced tomatoes

1 tablespoon paprika (preferably Hungarian)

2 tablespoons chopped fresh parsley *or* 1 teaspoon dried parsley flakes

1 teaspoon dried thyme

2 bay leaves

¼ cup sour cream, or to taste

Hot cooked egg noodles

Chopped fresh dill (optional)

1. Combine flour, 2 teaspoons salt and pepper in large resealable food storage bag. Add beef; toss to coat. Shake off any excess flour mixture.

2. Press Sauté; heat 2 tablespoons oil in pot. Add beef in two batches; cook until browned on all sides. Remove to plate.

3. Add remaining 1 tablespoon oil to pot, if necessary. Add shallots and garlic; cook and stir 2 minutes or until softened. Add tomatoes and paprika; cook and stir 2 minutes, scraping up browned bits on bottom of pot. Return beef and any juices to pot with parsley, thyme, bay leaves and remaining ½ teaspoon salt; mix well.

4. Secure lid and move pressure release valve to sealing or locked position. Cook at high pressure 35 minutes.

5. When cooking is complete, use natural release for 10 minutes, then release remaining pressure.

6. Press Sauté; cook 5 minutes or until stew has thickened slightly. Turn off heat. Remove and discard bay leaf. Stir in sour cream until blended. Serve over noodles; garnish with dill.

Makes 4 to 6 servings

Beef Pot Roast Dinner

2 cloves garlic, minced

1 teaspoon salt

1 teaspoon herbes de Provence*

1 teaspoon ground cumin

1 teaspoon ground sage

1 teaspoon black pepper

1 beef eye of round roast (about 2½ pounds), trimmed

2 tablespoons olive oil

1 cup beef broth

4 small turnips, peeled and cut into wedges

12 fresh brussels sprouts, trimmed

2 cups halved small new red potatoes

2 cups baby carrots

1 cup pearl onions, skins removed *or* 1 large onion, cut into wedges

Or substitute ¼ teaspoon each dried rosemary, thyme, sage and savory.

1. Combine garlic, salt, herbes de Provence, cumin, sage and pepper in small bowl; mix well. Rub spice mixture into all sides of beef.

2. Press Sauté; heat oil in pot. Add beef; cook about 5 minutes or until browned on all sides. Remove to plate. Add broth; stir to scrape up browned bits from bottom of pot. Place rack in pot; place beef on rack.

3. Secure lid and move pressure release valve to sealing or locked position. Cook at high pressure 50 minutes.

4. When cooking is complete, use natural release for 5 minutes, then release remaining pressure.

5. Add turnips, brussels sprouts, potatoes, carrots and onions to pot. Secure lid and move pressure release valve to sealing or locked position. Cook at high pressure 10 minutes.

6. When cooking is complete, press Cancel or Stop and use quick release. Serve beef and vegetables with cooking liquid or thicken sauce, if desired.

Makes 4 to 6 servings

Italian Short Ribs

2 tablespoons vegetable oil

3 pounds bone-in beef short ribs, trimmed and cut into 3-inch pieces

1 teaspoon Italian seasoning

¾ teaspoon salt

¼ teaspoon black pepper

1½ cups chopped leeks (2 to 3 leeks)

½ cup dry white wine

¾ cup pitted kalamata or oil-cured olives

1¼ cups prepared pasta sauce

Parmesan Polenta (recipe follows, optional)

1. Press Sauté; heat oil in pot. Add short ribs in batches; cook about 8 minutes or until browned on all sides. Remove to plate; season with Italian seasoning, salt and pepper. Drain off all but 1 tablespoon fat.

2. Add leeks to pot; cook and stir 2 minutes or until softened. Add wine; cook until almost evaporated, scraping up browned bits from bottom of pot. Return short ribs to pot with olives; pour pasta sauce over short ribs.

3. Secure lid and move pressure release valve to sealing or locked position. Cook at high pressure 30 minutes.

4. When cooking is complete, use natural release for 10 minutes, then release remaining pressure.

5. Meanwhile, prepare Parmesan Polenta, if desired. Serve ribs and sauce with polenta.

Makes 4 servings

Parmesan Polenta: Bring 2 cups water to a boil in large nonstick saucepan over medium-high heat. Gradually whisk in 1 cup instant polenta until smooth and thick. Stir in ½ cup grated Parmesan cheese. Season with salt and pepper.

Easy Meatballs

1 pound ground beef

1 egg, beaten

3 tablespoons Italian-seasoned dry bread crumbs

1 clove garlic, minced

1 teaspoon dried oregano

¾ teaspoon salt

¼ teaspoon black pepper

⅛ teaspoon ground red pepper

3 cups marinara or tomato-basil pasta sauce

Hot cooked spaghetti

Chopped fresh basil (optional)

Grated Parmesan cheese (optional)

1. Combine beef, egg, bread crumbs, garlic, oregano, salt, black pepper and red pepper in medium bowl; mix gently. Shape into 16 (1½-inch) meatballs.

2. Pour pasta sauce into pot. Add meatballs to sauce; turn to coat and submerge meatballs in sauce.

3. Secure lid and move pressure release valve to sealing or locked position. Cook at high pressure 8 minutes.

4. When cooking is complete, press Cancel or Stop and use quick release. Serve meatballs and sauce over spaghetti; top with basil and cheese, if desired.

Makes 4 servings

Beef Stew with a Coffee Kick

⅓ cup all-purpose flour

1 teaspoon salt

1 teaspoon dried marjoram

½ teaspoon garlic powder

½ teaspoon black pepper

2 pounds beef stew meat, cut into 1-inch pieces

2 to 3 tablespoons vegetable oil, divided

3 small onions, cut into wedges

¾ cup strong brewed coffee, at room temperature

1 can (about 14 ounces) diced tomatoes

1 bay leaf

2 cups diced peeled potatoes (½-inch pieces)

4 stalks celery, cut into ½-inch slices

4 medium carrots, cut into ½-inch slices

1. Combine flour, salt, marjoram, garlic powder and pepper in large resealable food storage bag. Add beef; toss to coat; Shake off any excess flour mixture.

2. Press Sauté; heat 2 tablespoons oil in pot. Add beef in two batches; cook until browned on all sides. Remove to plate.

3. Add remaining 1 tablespoon oil to pot, if necessary. Add onions; cook and stir 3 minutes or until softened. Add coffee; cook and stir 1 minute, scraping up browned bits from bottom of pot. Return beef to pot. Stir in tomatoes and bay leaf.

4. Secure lid and move pressure release valve to sealing or locked position. Cook at high pressure 25 minutes.

5. When cooking is complete, use natural release for 5 minutes, then release remaining pressure. Add potatoes, celery and carrots to pot. Secure lid and move pressure release valve to sealing or locked position. Cook at high pressure 12 minutes.

6. When cooking is complete, press Cancel or Stop and use quick release. Remove and discard bay leaf. Let stew cool in pot 5 minutes, stirring occasionally. (Stew will thicken as it cools.)

Makes 6 servings

Onion-Wine Pot Roast

1 pound yellow onions, cut in half and thinly sliced

1 teaspoon salt

½ teaspoon black pepper

1 boneless beef chuck roast (about 3 pounds), trimmed

½ cup dry red wine, such as cabernet sauvignon or merlot

1. Place half of onions in pot; sprinkle with half of salt and pepper. Top with beef, remaining onions, salt and pepper. Pour in wine.

2. Secure lid and move pressure release valve to sealing or locked position. Cook at high pressure 70 minutes.

3. When cooking is complete, use natural release for 10 minutes, then release remaining pressure. Remove beef to cutting board; cover loosely to keep warm.

4. Press Sauté; cook about 10 minutes or until cooking liquid is reduced by one third.

Makes 4 to 6 servings

One-Pot Chili Mac

1 pound ground beef

1 cup chopped onion

1 clove garlic, minced

1 tablespoon chili powder

½ teaspoon dried oregano

½ teaspoon ground cumin

¼ teaspoon red pepper flakes

2 cups uncooked macaroni

1 can (about 14 ounces) diced tomatoes

¼ cup water

1 teaspoon salt

¼ teaspoon black pepper

1. Press Sauté; add beef, onion and garlic to pot. Cook about 6 minutes or until beef is no longer pink, stirring frequently.

2. Add chili powder, oregano, cumin and red pepper flakes to pot; cook and stir 1 minute. Stir in macaroni, tomatoes, water, salt and black pepper; mix well.

3. Secure lid and move pressure release valve to sealing or locked position. Cook at high pressure 5 minutes.

4. When cooking is complete, press Cancel or Stop and use quick release.

Makes 4 servings

Brisket with Vegetables

1 tablespoon vegetable oil

1 beef brisket (4 to 5 pounds), trimmed

2 onions, thinly sliced

4 cloves garlic, minced

2 teaspoons dried thyme

½ teaspoon ground coriander

1 cup beef broth

1 teaspoon salt

½ teaspoon black pepper

2 pounds red potatoes, quartered

1 pound baby carrots

3 tablespoons water

2 tablespoons all-purpose flour

1. Press Sauté; heat oil in pot. Add brisket; cook until browned on all sides. Remove to plate. Add onions to pot; cook and stir 3 minutes or until softened. Add garlic, thyme and coriander; cook and stir 1 minute. Add broth, salt and pepper; cook and stir 1 minute, scraping up browned bits from bottom of pot. Return brisket to pot.

2. Secure lid and move pressure release valve to sealing or locked position. Cook at high pressure 60 minutes.

3. When cooking is complete, use natural release for 10 minutes, then release remaining pressure.

4. Add potatoes and carrots to pot. Secure lid and move pressure release valve to sealing or locked position. Cook at high pressure 10 minutes. When cooking is complete, use natural release for 10 minutes, then release remaining pressure. Remove brisket and vegetables to platter; cover loosely to keep warm.

5. Stir water into flour in small bowl until smooth. Add ¼ cup hot cooking liquid; stir until blended. Press Sauté; add flour mixture to remaining cooking liquid in pot. Cook and stir 3 to 4 minutes or until sauce is thickened.

6. Slice brisket across the grain. Serve brisket and vegetables with sauce.

Makes 8 servings

Saucy BBQ Short Ribs

¾ cup regular cola (not diet)

1 can (6 ounces) tomato paste

⅓ cup plus 1 tablespoon honey, divided

⅓ cup cider vinegar

1 teaspoon salt

1 teaspoon black pepper

2 cloves garlic, minced

Dash hot pepper sauce (optional)

4 pounds bone-in beef short ribs, trimmed and cut into 2-inch pieces

1. Combine cola, tomato paste, ⅓ cup honey, vinegar, salt, black pepper, garlic and hot pepper sauce, if desired, in pot; mix well. Add short ribs; turn to coat with sauce.

2. Secure lid and move pressure release valve to sealing or locked position. Cook at high pressure 30 minutes.

3. When cooking is complete, use natural release for 10 minutes, then release remaining pressure. Remove short ribs to plate; cover loosely to keep warm.

4. Skim excess fat from surface of sauce. Press Sauté; cook sauce 10 to 15 minutes or until reduced by one third. Add remaining 1 tablespoon honey; cook and stir 1 minute. Brush short ribs with sauce.

Makes 4 servings

Tip: For a thicker sauce, stir 2 tablespoons water into 2 tablespoons cornstarch in a small bowl until smooth. Add to the sauce with the honey in Step 4; cook and stir 1 minute or until thickened.

PORK & LAMB

Maple Spice Rubbed Ribs

3 teaspoons chili powder, divided

1¼ teaspoons ground coriander

1¼ teaspoons garlic powder, divided

¾ teaspoon salt

½ teaspoon black pepper

3 to 3½ pounds pork baby back ribs, trimmed and cut into 4-rib pieces

4 tablespoons maple syrup, divided

1 can (8 ounces) tomato sauce

¼ teaspoon ground cinnamon

¼ teaspoon ground ginger

1. Combine 1½ teaspoons chili powder, coriander, ¾ teaspoon garlic powder, salt and pepper in small bowl; mix well. Brush ribs with 2 tablespoons maple syrup; rub with spice mixture. Place ribs in pot.

2. Combine tomato sauce, remaining 2 tablespoons maple syrup, 1½ teaspoons chili powder, ½ teaspoon garlic powder, cinnamon and ginger in medium bowl; mix well. Pour over ribs in pot; stir to coat ribs with sauce.

3. Secure lid and move pressure release valve to sealing or locked position. Cook at high pressure 25 minutes.

4. When cooking is complete, use natural release for 10 minutes, then release remaining pressure. Remove ribs to plate; cover loosely to keep warm.

5. Press Sauté; cook sauce about 10 minutes or until thickened. Brush ribs with sauce; serve remaining sauce on the side.

Makes 4 servings

Chipotle Pork Tacos

1 tablespoon vegetable oil

1 cup finely chopped onion

1 medium onion, thinly sliced

4 cloves garlic, minced

½ teaspoon ground cumin

1 can (8 ounces) tomato sauce

¼ cup water

3 tablespoons cider vinegar, divided

2 chipotle peppers in adobo sauce, finely chopped

1 teaspoon salt

2½ pounds boneless pork shoulder, trimmed and cut into 3-inch pieces

Roasted Green Onions (recipe follows, optional)

16 (6-inch) corn tortillas

1. Press Sauté; heat oil in pot. Add onion; cook and stir 3 minutes or until softened. Add garlic and cumin; cook and stir 30 seconds. Stir in tomato sauce, water, 2 tablespoons vinegar, chipotle peppers and salt; mix well. Add pork to pot, pressing into liquid.

2. Secure lid and move pressure release valve to sealing or locked position. Cook at high pressure 45 minutes.

3. When cooking is complete, use natural release for 10 minutes, then release remaining pressure. Remove pork to plate.

4. Skim excess fat from surface of sauce. Stir in remaining 1 tablespoon vinegar. Press Sauté; cook sauce about 15 minutes or until reduced by half and slightly thickened, stirring occasionally.

5. Meanwhile, prepare Roasted Green Onions, if desired. Shred pork into bite-sized pieces. Combine pork and 1 cup sauce in large bowl; toss to coat. Add additional sauce if necessary.

6. Heat tortillas over stovetop burner or grill about 15 seconds per side or until lightly charred. Fill tortillas with pork mixture and Roasted Green Onions.

Makes 6 to 8 servings

Roasted Green Onions: Preheat oven to 425°F. Trim 16 green onions; place on large baking sheet. Drizzle with 1 tablespoon olive oil; toss gently to coat. Arrange in single layer; roast 10 minutes. Sprinkle with salt.

Greek-Style Lamb Chops

3 cloves garlic, minced

1 teaspoon Greek seasoning

1 teaspoon salt

1 teaspoon black pepper

4 bone-in lamb shoulder chops (¾ to 1 inch thick, about 2 pounds)

3 tablespoons olive oil

1 large onion, sliced

½ cup dry white wine

3 plum tomatoes, each cut into 6 wedges

½ cup pitted kalamata olives

½ cup chicken broth

Chopped fresh parsley

1. Combine garlic, Greek seasoning, salt and pepper in small bowl; mix well. Rub spice mixture into both sides of lamb chops.

2. Press Sauté; heat oil in pot. Add lamb chops in two batches; cook about 8 minutes or until browned on both sides. Remove to plate. Add onion and wine; cook and stir 3 minutes or until onion is softened and wine is almost evaporated, scraping up browned bits from bottom of pot. Stir in tomatoes, olives and broth; mix well. Return lamb to pot, pressing into tomato mixture.

3. Secure lid and move pressure release valve to sealing or locked position. Cook at high pressure 12 minutes.

4. When cooking is complete, use natural release for 10 minutes, then release remaining pressure. Remove lamb and tomatoes to clean plate; cover loosely to keep warm.

5. Press Sauté; cook sauce 10 to 15 minutes or until reduced by one third. Serve sauce over lamb and vegetables; sprinkle with parsley.

Makes 4 servings

Tip: To make your own Greek seasoning, combine 1½ teaspoons dried oregano, 1 teaspoon dried mint, 1 teaspoon dried thyme, ½ teaspoon dried basil, ½ teaspoon dried marjoram, ¼ teaspoon onion powder, and ¼ teaspoon garlic powder in a small bowl; mix well. Store in an airtight container.

Pork Roast with Tart Cherries

3 teaspoons grated horseradish, divided

2 teaspoons ground coriander

¾ teaspoon salt

½ teaspoon black pepper

1 tablespoon olive oil

1 boneless pork loin roast (about 2 pounds), trimmed

1 can (about 14 ounces) pitted tart cherries, undrained

¼ cup dry sherry, Madeira or white wine

4 teaspoons grated orange peel

1 tablespoon packed brown sugar

1 tablespoon Dijon mustard

⅛ teaspoon ground cloves

Fresh Italian parsley sprigs (optional)

Orange slices (optional)

1. Combine 2 teaspoons horseradish, coriander, salt and pepper in small bowl; mix well. Press Sauté; heat oil in pot. Add pork; cook about 10 minutes or until browned on all sides. Remove to plate; rub horseradish mixture into all sides of pork.

2. Drain cherries, reserving ¼ cup liquid. Add cherries, reserved cherry liquid and sherry to pot; cook about 4 minutes or until half of liquid is evaporated, scraping up browned bits from bottom of pot. Place rack in pot; place pork on rack.

3. Secure lid and move pressure release valve to sealing or locked position. Cook at high pressure 25 minutes.

4. When cooking is complete, use natural release for 10 minutes, then release remaining pressure. Remove pork to plate; cover loosely to keep warm.

5. Strain cooking liquid into medium bowl, reserving cherries. Return liquid to pot. Press Sauté; stir in orange peel, brown sugar, mustard, remaining 1 teaspoon horseradish and cloves. Cook 10 minutes or until sauce is slightly thickened, stirring occasionally. Stir in reserved cherries. Serve sauce with pork; garnish with parsley and orange slices.

Makes 4 to 6 servings

Three-Bean Chili with Chorizo

½ cup dried pinto beans, soaked 8 hours or overnight

½ cup dried kidney beans, soaked 8 hours or overnight

½ cup dried black beans, soaked 8 hours or overnight

2 Mexican chorizo sausages (about 6 ounces each), casings removed

1 tablespoon vegetable oil

1 large onion, chopped

1 tablespoon salt

1 tablespoon tomato paste

1 tablespoon minced garlic

1 tablespoon chili powder

1 tablespoon ancho chili powder

1 teaspoon chipotle chili powder

2 teaspoons ground cumin

1 teaspoon ground coriander

1 can (about 28 ounces) crushed tomatoes

2 cups water

Chopped fresh cilantro (optional)

1. Drain and rinse beans. Press Sauté; add chorizo to pot. Cook 3 to 4 minutes, stirring to break up meat. Remove to bowl.

2. Heat oil in pot. Add onion; cook and stir 3 minutes or until softened. Add salt, tomato paste, garlic, chili powders, cumin and coriander; cook and stir 1 minute. Stir in tomatoes, water, beans and chorizo; mix well.

3. Secure lid and move pressure release valve to sealing or locked position. Cook at high pressure 20 minutes.

4. When cooking is complete, use natural release for 10 minutes, then release remaining pressure. Garnish with cilantro.

Makes 6 to 8 servings

Canton Pork Stew

1 cup chicken broth

¼ cup dry sherry

3 tablespoons soy sauce

1 tablespoon hoisin sauce

1½ tablespoons cornstarch

2 tablespoons vegetable oil

1½ pounds boneless pork shoulder, trimmed and cut into 1-inch pieces

1 large onion, chopped

3 cloves garlic, minced

1 teaspoon Chinese five-spice powder*

½ teaspoon salt

2 cups baby carrots

1 large green bell pepper, cut into 1-inch pieces

Chinese five-spice powder is a blend of cinnamon, cloves, fennel seed, anise and Szechuan peppercorns. It is available in most supermarkets and in Asian grocery stores.

1. Combine broth, sherry, soy sauce and hoisin sauce in medium bowl; mix well. Stir 3 tablespoons broth mixture into cornstarch in small bowl until smooth; set aside to thicken stew after cooking.

2. Press Sauté; heat oil in pot. Add pork in two batches; cook until browned on all sides. Remove to plate.

3. Add onion to pot; cook and stir 3 minutes or until softened. Add garlic, five-spice powder and salt; cook and stir 30 seconds. Add broth mixture; cook and stir 1 minute, scraping up browned bits from bottom of pot. Return pork to pot.

4. Secure lid and move pressure release valve to sealing or locked position. Cook at high pressure 15 minutes.

5. When cooking is complete, press Cancel or Stop and use quick release. Add carrots and bell pepper to pot. Secure lid and move pressure release valve to sealing or locked position. Cook at high pressure 2 minutes. When cooking is complete, press Cancel or Stop and use quick release.

6. Stir reserved cornstarch mixture. Press Sauté; add cornstarch mixture to pot, stirring constantly. Cook and stir about 1 minute or until thickened.

Makes 6 servings

Beer Barbecued Pulled Pork Sandwiches

1 tablespoon chili powder

½ teaspoon salt

¼ teaspoon black pepper

2 pounds boneless pork shoulder, trimmed and cut into 3-inch pieces

1 tablespoon vegetable oil, divided

1 cup chopped onion

1 cup ale or dark beer*

⅓ cup ketchup

¼ cup chicken broth

3 tablespoons honey

2 tablespoons cider vinegar

2 tablespoons whole grain mustard

8 sandwich rolls, split

Bread-and-butter pickle chips

For best flavor, do not use light beer.

1. Combine chili powder, salt, and pepper in small bowl; mix well. Rub spice mixture into all sides of pork.

2. Press Sauté; heat oil in pot. Add pork in batches; cook about 8 minutes or until browned on all sides. Remove to plate. Add onion, beer, ketchup, broth, honey, vinegar and mustard; cook and stir 2 minutes, scraping up browned bits from bottom of pot. Return pork to pot, pressing into beer mixture.

3. Secure lid and move pressure release valve to sealing or locked position. Cook at high pressure 45 minutes.

4. When cooking is complete, use natural release for 10 minutes, then release remaining pressure. Remove pork to clean plate.

5. Skim excess fat from surface of sauce. Press Sauté; cook sauce about 10 minutes or until reduced by one third. Meanwhile, shred pork into bite-size pieces when cool enough to handle.

6. Combine pork and 1 cup sauce in large bowl; toss to coat. Add additional sauce if necessary. Serve pork on rolls with pickles.

Makes 8 servings

Pork Loin with Apples and Onions

2 tablespoons vegetable oil

1 bone-in or boneless pork loin roast (about 3 pounds), trimmed

2 medium onions, chopped

2 sweet-tart apples such as Braeburn, Honeycrisp or Jonagold, peeled and thinly sliced

1 cup lager beer

2 tablespoons packed brown sugar

1 teaspoon ground ginger

½ teaspoon salt

½ teaspoon ground cinnamon

½ teaspoon black pepper

⅛ teaspoon ground red pepper

1. Press Sauté; heat oil in pot. Add pork; cook about 8 minutes or until browned on all sides. Remove to plate.

2. Add onions to pot; cook and stir 5 minutes or until lightly browned. Add apples, beer, brown sugar, ginger, salt, cinnamon, black pepper and red pepper; cook and stir 1 minute, scraping up browned bits from bottom of pot. Return pork to pot.

3. Secure lid and move pressure release valve to sealing or locked position. Cook at high pressure 35 minutes.

4. When cooking is complete, use natural release for 10 minutes, then release remaining pressure. Remove pork to cutting board; cover loosely to keep warm.

5. Press Sauté; cook sauce about 10 minutes or until reduced by one third, stirring occasionally. Serve sauce with pork.

Makes 4 servings

Tip: Pork should be cooked to an internal temperature of at least 145°F. Use an instant-read thermometer to check the temperature of the pork after releasing the pressure. If necessary, cook an additional few minutes.

Spicy-Sweet Lamb Tagine

¾ cup dried chickpeas, soaked 8 hours or overnight

1 tablespoon olive oil

2 pounds boneless lamb shoulder or leg, cut into 1½-inch pieces

3 medium onions, each cut into 8 wedges

3 cloves garlic, minced

2 teaspoons ground ginger

2 teaspoons ground cinnamon

1 teaspoon black pepper

1½ cups water

1 can (about 14 ounces) diced tomatoes

2 teaspoons salt

1 small butternut squash, peeled and cut into 1-inch pieces (3 to 4 cups)

1 cup chopped pitted prunes

2 medium zucchini, halved lengthwise and cut crosswise into ½-inch slices

Saffron Couscous (recipe follows, optional)

¼ cup chopped fresh cilantro or parsley

1. Drain and rinse chickpeas. Press Sauté; heat oil in pot. Add lamb in two batches; cook about 5 minutes or until browned on all sides. Remove to plate.

2. Add onions, garlic, ginger, cinnamon and pepper to pot; cook and stir 30 seconds or until spices are fragrant. Add water; cook and stir 2 minutes, scraping up browned bits from bottom of pot. Stir in tomatoes, chickpeas and salt; mix well. Return lamb to pot.

3. Secure lid and move pressure release valve to sealing or locked position. Cook at high pressure 15 minutes. When cooking is complete, press Cancel or Stop and use quick release.

4. Add butternut squash and prunes to pot. Secure lid and move pressure release valve to sealing or locked position. Cook at high pressure 3 minutes. When cooking is complete, press Cancel or Stop and use quick release.

5. Press Sauté; add zucchini to pot. Cook 4 minutes or until zucchini is crisp-tender, stirring occasionally.

6. Meanwhile, prepare Saffron Couscous, if desired. Serve stew over couscous. Garnish with cilantro.

Makes 4 to 6 servings

Saffron Couscous: Combine 2¼ cups water, 1 tablespoon butter, ¼ teaspoon salt and ¼ teaspoon crushed saffron threads in medium saucepan; bring to a boil over high heat. Stir in 1½ cups uncooked couscous. Remove from heat; cover and let stand 5 minutes or until liquid is absorbed. Fluff with fork.

Honey Ginger Ribs

2 pounds pork baby back ribs, trimmed and cut into 2-rib pieces

4 green onions, chopped

½ cup hoisin sauce, divided

3 tablespoons dry sherry or rice wine

2 tablespoons soy sauce

2 tablespoons honey

1 tablespoon cider vinegar

1 tablespoon packed brown sugar

1 teaspoon minced fresh ginger

2 cloves garlic, minced

¼ teaspoon Chinese five-spice powder*

⅓ cup chicken or beef broth

2 tablespoons cornstarch

Sesame seeds (optional)

Chinese five-spice powder is a blend of cinnamon, cloves, fennel seed, anise and Szechuan peppercorns. It is available in the spice section of most supermarkets and at Asian grocery stores.

1. Place ribs in large resealable food storage bag. Combine green onions, ¼ cup hoisin sauce, sherry, soy sauce, honey, vinegar, brown sugar, ginger, garlic and five-spice powder in medium bowl; mix well. Pour marinade over ribs. Seal bag; turn to coat. Refrigerate 2 to 4 hours or overnight, turning occasionally.

2. Pour broth into pot; add ribs and marinade. Secure lid and move pressure release valve to sealing or locked position. Cook at high pressure 25 minutes.

3. When cooking is complete, use natural release for 10 minutes, then release remaining pressure. Remove ribs to plate; cover loosely to keep warm.

4. Skim excess fat from surface of sauce. Stir 2 tablespoons sauce into cornstarch in small bowl until smooth. Press Sauté; add cornstarch mixture to pot, stirring constantly. Cook and stir sauce about 2 minutes or until slightly thickened. Add remaining ¼ cup hoisin sauce; cook and stir until heated through.

5. Brush sauce over ribs before serving. Sprinkle with sesame seeds, if desired.

Makes 4 servings

Chili Verde

1 tablespoon vegetable oil

1 pound boneless pork loin, cut into 1-inch pieces

1 onion, halved and thinly sliced

1 pound tomatillos, husks removed, rinsed and coarsely chopped

6 cloves garlic, minced

1 teaspoon ground cumin

1 can (about 15 ounces) Great Northern beans, drained and rinsed

1 can (4 ounces) diced green chiles

1 teaspoon salt

¼ teaspoon black pepper

¼ cup chopped fresh cilantro

1. Press Sauté; heat oil in pot. Add pork; cook about 6 minutes or until browned on all sides, stirring occasionally. Remove to plate.

2. Add onion to pot; cook and stir 3 minutes or until softened. Add tomatillos, garlic and cumin; cook and stir 3 minutes, scraping up browned bits from bottom of pot. Stir in beans, chiles, salt, pepper and pork; mix well.

3. Secure lid and move pressure release valve to sealing or locked position. Cook at high pressure 8 minutes.

4. When cooking is complete, use natural release for 10 minutes, then release remaining pressure. Stir in cilantro.

Makes 4 servings

Jerk Pork and Sweet Potato Stew

2 tablespoons all-purpose flour

1 teaspoon salt

¼ teaspoon black pepper

1¼ pounds boneless pork shoulder, cut into 1-inch pieces

2 tablespoons vegetable oil

4 tablespoons minced green onions, divided

1 small jalapeño pepper,* seeded and minced

1 clove garlic, minced

⅛ teaspoon ground allspice

1 cup chicken broth

1 large sweet potato, peeled and cut into ¾-inch pieces

1 cup thawed frozen corn

1 tablespoon lime juice

Hot cooked rice (optional)

*Jalapeño peppers can sting and irritate the skin, so wear rubber gloves when handling and do not touch your eyes.

1. Combine flour, salt and black pepper in large resealable food storage bag. Add pork; seal bag and shake to coat.

2. Press Sauté; heat oil in pot. Add pork in two batches, cook about 5 minutes or until browned on all sides. Remove to plate.

3. Add 2 tablespoons green onions, jalapeño, garlic and allspice to pot; cook and stir 30 seconds. Stir in broth, scraping up browned bits from bottom of pot. Return pork to pot.

4. Secure lid and move pressure release valve to sealing or locked position. Cook at high pressure 18 minutes.

5. When cooking is complete, press Cancel or Stop and use quick release. Stir in sweet potato. Secure lid and move pressure release valve to sealing or locked position. Cook at high pressure 2 minutes.

6. When cooking is complete, press Cancel or Stop and use quick release. Stir in corn, remaining 2 tablespoons green onions and lime juice; let stand 2 minutes or until corn is heated through. Serve with rice, if desired.

Makes 4 servings

Chili Spiced Pork Loin

1 boneless pork loin roast
(2 to 2½ pounds), trimmed

1¼ cups orange juice, divided

1 cup chopped onion

2 cloves garlic, minced

1 tablespoon cider vinegar

1½ teaspoons chili powder

1 teaspoon salt

¼ teaspoon dried thyme

¼ teaspoon ground cumin

¼ teaspoon ground cinnamon

⅛ teaspoon ground allspice

⅛ teaspoon ground cloves

2 tablespoons olive oil

Fruit Chutney
(recipe follows, optional)

1. Place pork in large resealable food storage bag or glass dish. Combine ¼ cup orange juice, onion, garlic, vinegar, chili powder, salt, thyme, cumin, cinnamon, allspice and cloves in small bowl; mix well. Pour marinade over pork; seal bag and turn to coat. Refrigerate 2 to 4 hours or overnight.

2. Remove pork from marinade; reserve marinade. Press Sauté; heat oil in pot. Add pork; cook about 6 minutes or until browned on all sides. Add remaining 1 cup orange juice and reserved marinade; stir to scrape up browned bits from bottom of pot.

3. Secure lid and move pressure release valve to sealing or locked position. Cook at high pressure 20 minutes.

4. When cooking is complete, use natural release for 10 minutes, then release remaining pressure. Remove pork to cutting board; cover loosely to keep warm. Let stand 10 minutes before slicing.

5. Meanwhile, prepare Fruit Chutney, if desired. Or press Sauté and heat remaining cooking liquid to a boil; cook until sauce is reduced by one third. Serve with pork.

Makes 4 servings

Fruit Chutney: Add ¼ cup apricot preserves or orange marmalade to cooking liquid after removing pork from pot. Press Sauté; cook 10 minutes, stirring occasionally. Add 1 diced mango, ½ cup diced fresh pineapple, 2 minced green onions and 1 tablespoon minced jalapeño pepper; cook and stir 5 minutes. Serve with pork.

Italian Tomato-Braised Lamb

1 can (about 28 ounces) whole plum tomatoes, undrained

4 bone-in lamb shoulder chops (¾ to 1 inch thick, about 2 pounds)

1½ teaspoons dried oregano

½ teaspoon salt

¼ teaspoon black pepper

2 tablespoons olive oil

2 onions, cut into quarters and thinly sliced

3 cloves garlic, minced

2 tablespoons red wine vinegar

3 to 4 sprigs fresh rosemary

Hot cooked polenta or pasta (optional)

1. Drain tomatoes, reserving 1 cup juice. Coarsely chop tomatoes. (Tomatoes can also be broken up with hands or cut with scissors in can.)

2. Season both sides of lamb with oregano, salt and pepper. Press Sauté; heat oil in pot. Add onions and garlic; cook and stir 3 minutes or until softened. Add tomatoes, reserved 1 cup juice and vinegar; cook and stir 1 minute. Add lamb and rosemary to pot, pressing into liquid.

3. Secure lid and move pressure release valve to sealing or locked position. Cook at high pressure 12 minutes.

4. When cooking is complete, use natural release for 10 minutes, then release remaining pressure. Remove lamb to plate; cover loosely to keep warm. Remove and discard rosemary sprigs.

5. Press Sauté; cook sauce 5 to 10 minutes or until reduced by one third. Serve sauce with lamb and polenta, if desired.

Makes 4 servings

Ale'd Pork and Sauerkraut

2 teaspoons paprika

1 teaspoon garlic powder

½ teaspoon salt

¼ teaspoon black pepper

1 boneless pork shoulder or pork butt roast (about 3½ pounds), trimmed

1½ tablespoons vegetable oil

1 jar (32 ounces) sauerkraut, drained

1 bottle or can (12 ounces) ale or dark beer

1 tablespoon sugar

1. Combine paprika, garlic powder, salt and pepper in small bowl; mix well. Rub spice mixture into all sides of pork.

2. Press Sauté; heat oil in pot. Add pork; cook about 8 minutes or until browned on all sides. Remove to plate.

3. Add sauerkraut, ale and sugar to pot; cook and stir 2 minutes, scraping up browned bits from bottom of pot. Return pork to pot, pressing into sauerkraut mixture.

4. Secure lid and move pressure release valve to sealing or locked position. Cook at high pressure 45 minutes.

5. When cooking is complete, use natural release for 10 minutes, then release remaining pressure. Remove pork to cutting board; cover loosely to keep warm. Let stand 5 minutes before slicing. Serve with sauerkraut and cooking liquid remaining in pot.

Makes 4 to 6 servings

POULTRY

Indian-Style Apricot Chicken

2½ pounds bone-in skinless
  chicken thighs

½ teaspoon salt

¼ teaspoon black pepper

1 tablespoon vegetable oil

1 large onion, chopped

½ cup chicken broth, divided

1 tablespoon grated fresh ginger

2 cloves garlic, minced

½ teaspoon ground cinnamon

⅛ teaspoon ground allspice

1 can (about 14 ounces) diced
  tomatoes

1 package (8 ounces) dried
  apricots

  Pinch saffron threads (optional)

  Chopped fresh Italian parsley
  (optional)

1. Season both sides of chicken with ½ teaspoon salt and ¼ teaspoon pepper. Press Sauté; heat oil in pot. Add chicken in batches; cook about 8 minutes or until browned on both sides. Remove to plate.

2. Add onion and 2 tablespoons broth to pot; cook and stir 5 minutes or until onion is translucent, scraping up browned bits from bottom of pot. Add ginger, garlic, cinnamon and allspice; cook and stir 30 seconds or until fragrant. Stir in tomatoes, apricots, remaining broth and saffron, if desired; mix well. Return chicken to pot, pressing into liquid.

3. Secure lid and move pressure release valve to sealing or locked position. Cook at high pressure 11 minutes.

4. When cooking is complete, press Cancel or Stop and use quick release. Season with additional salt and pepper. Garnish with parsley.

Makes 4 to 6 servings

Lemon Rosemary Chicken and Potatoes

4 bone-in skinless chicken breasts (about 8 ounces each)

2 pounds small red potatoes, cut into halves or quarters (1½-inch pieces)

1 large onion, cut into 2-inch pieces

½ cup lemon juice

6 tablespoons olive oil

6 cloves garlic, minced

2 tablespoons plus 1 teaspoon finely chopped fresh rosemary leaves *or* 2¼ teaspoons dried rosemary

2 teaspoons grated lemon peel

1½ teaspoons salt

½ teaspoon black pepper

1 tablespoon vegetable oil

½ cup chicken broth

1. Place chicken in large resealable food storage bag. Place potatoes and onion in another resealable bag. Combine lemon juice, olive oil, garlic, rosemary, lemon peel, 1½ teaspoons salt and pepper in small bowl; mix well. Pour half of marinade (about 6 tablespoons) over chicken; pour remaining marinade over potatoes and onion. Seal bags and turn to coat. Refrigerate 2 hours or overnight.

2. Remove chicken from marinade; discard marinade. Press Sauté; heat vegetable oil in pot. Add chicken in batches; cook about 8 minutes or until browned on all sides. Remove to plate.

3. Remove potatoes and onion from marinade; reserve marinade. Add vegetables to pot; cook and stir 3 minutes, scraping up browned bits from bottom of pot. Arrange chicken on top of vegetables; pour reserved marinade and broth over chicken.

4. Secure lid and move pressure release valve to sealing or locked position. Cook at high pressure 9 minutes.

5. When cooking is complete, press Cancel or Stop and use quick release. Remove chicken and vegetables to platter; cover loosely to keep warm.

6. Skim excess fat from surface of cooking liquid. Press Sauté; cook about 5 minutes until sauce is slightly reduced. Season vegetables with additional salt, if desired. Serve sauce over chicken and vegetables.

Makes 4 servings

Chili Turkey Breast with Cilantro-Lime Rice

TURKEY

1½ tablespoons chili powder

2 teaspoons dried oregano

1½ teaspoons ground cumin

½ teaspoon red pepper flakes

½ teaspoon salt

½ teaspoon black pepper

1 bone-in turkey breast (about 4 pounds), skin removed

1 cup chicken broth

RICE

1½ cups uncooked long grain rice

2 medium red bell peppers, chopped

1 cup chopped green onions

¾ cup water

½ cup chopped fresh cilantro

2 tablespoons lime juice

1 tablespoon grated lime peel

1 teaspoon olive oil

½ teaspoon salt

½ teaspoon ground turmeric (optional)

1. Combine chili powder, oregano, cumin, red pepper flakes, salt and black pepper in small bowl; mix well. Rub spice mixture into all sides of turkey. Pour broth into pot. Place rack in pot; place turkey on rack.

2. Secure lid and move pressure release valve to sealing or locked position. Cook at high pressure 35 minutes.

3. When cooking is complete, use natural release for 10 minutes, then release remaining pressure. Remove turkey to cutting board; cover loosely to keep warm. Reserve ¾ cup cooking liquid for rice; discard remaining liquid. Wipe out pot with paper towels.

4. Rinse rice well; drain in fine-mesh strainer. Combine rice, bell peppers, green onions, water, reserved ¾ cup cooking liquid, cilantro, lime juice, lime peel, oil, salt and turmeric, if desired, in pot; mix well.

5. Secure lid and move pressure release valve to sealing or locked position. Cook at high pressure 4 minutes.

6. When cooking is complete, use natural release for 10 minutes, then release remaining pressure. Fluff rice gently with fork before serving with turkey.

Makes 6 to 8 servings

Hearty Chicken Chili

1 tablespoon vegetable oil

1 onion, finely chopped

1 jalapeño pepper,* minced

1 clove garlic, minced

1½ teaspoons chili powder

¾ teaspoon salt

½ teaspoon ground cumin

½ teaspoon dried oregano

½ teaspoon black pepper

¼ teaspoon red pepper flakes (optional)

1 cup chicken broth

1½ pounds boneless skinless chicken thighs, cut into 1-inch pieces

2 cans (about 15 ounces each) hominy, rinsed and drained

1 can (about 15 ounces) pinto beans, rinsed and drained

1 tablespoon all-purpose flour (optional)

Chopped fresh cilantro

Lime wedges (optional)

*Jalapeño peppers can sting and irritate the skin, so wear rubber gloves when handling peppers and do not touch your eyes.

1. Press Sauté; heat oil in pot. Add onion; cook and stir 3 minutes or until softened. Add jalapeño, garlic, chili powder, salt, cumin, oregano, black pepper and red pepper flakes, if desired; cook and stir 30 seconds. Stir in broth; cook 1 minute. Add chicken, hominy and beans; mix well.

2. Secure lid and move pressure release valve to sealing or locked position. Cook at high pressure 6 minutes.

3. When cooking is complete, use natural release for 10 minutes, then release remaining pressure.

4. For thicker chili, stir 1 tablespoon flour into 3 tablespoons cooking liquid in small bowl until smooth. Press Sauté; add flour mixture to chili. Cook about 5 minutes or until thickened, stirring occasionally. Sprinkle with cilantro; serve with lime wedges, if desired.

Makes 4 servings

Italian Country-Style Chicken

1 cup boiling water

½ cup dried porcini mushrooms
(about ½ ounce)

⅓ cup all-purpose flour

1 teaspoon salt

½ teaspoon black pepper

1 cut-up whole chicken
(3½ to 4 pounds)*

3 tablespoons olive oil

3 ounces pancetta,** chopped
(about ½ cup)

1 medium onion, chopped

2 carrots, cut diagonally into
¼-inch slices

3 cloves garlic, minced

1 tablespoon tomato paste

1 cup pitted green Italian olives

*Or purchase 2 leg quarters and 2 breasts and
cut each into two pieces.

**Or substitute 3 ounces bacon.

1. Combine boiling water and mushrooms in medium bowl; let stand 15 to 20 minutes or until mushrooms are softened.

2. Meanwhile, combine flour, salt and pepper in large resealable food storage bag. Add 1 or 2 pieces of chicken at a time; toss to coat. Discard any remaining flour mixture.

3. Press Sauté; heat 1 tablespoon oil in pot. Add chicken in batches; cook until browned on both sides. Remove to plate. Pour off all but 1 tablespoon fat.

4. Drain mushrooms, reserving liquid. Chop mushrooms. Add pancetta, onion and carrots to pot; cook and stir 5 minutes. Add garlic and tomato paste; cook and stir 1 minute. Add reserved mushroom liquid; cook 2 minutes, scraping up browned bits from bottom of pot. Stir in mushrooms; mix well. Return chicken to pot.

5. Secure lid and move pressure release valve to sealing or locked position. Cook at high pressure 10 minutes.

6. When cooking is complete, press Cancel or Stop and use quick release. Remove chicken to platter; cover loosely to keep warm.

7. Press Sauté. Add olives; cook about 2 minutes or until heated through and sauce is slightly thickened, stirring frequently. Season with additional salt and pepper, if desired. Pour sauce over chicken.

Makes 4 servings

Turkey Ropa Vieja

1 tablespoon olive oil

1 onion, thinly sliced

1 green bell pepper, chopped

1 clove garlic, minced

¾ teaspoon ground cumin

½ teaspoon dried oregano

2 medium tomatoes, chopped

1 can (8 ounces) tomato sauce

⅓ cup sliced pimiento-stuffed green olives

½ teaspoon salt

¼ teaspoon black pepper

1 pound turkey tenderloins (2 large or 3 small) *or* 1½ pounds boneless turkey breast, cut into 3 to 4 pieces

1 tablespoon lemon juice

Hot cooked rice and beans (optional)

1. Press Sauté; heat oil in pot. Add onion and bell pepper; cook and stir 3 minutes or until softened. Add garlic, cumin and oregano; cook and stir 30 seconds. Stir in tomatoes, tomato sauce, olives, salt and black pepper; mix well. Add turkey to pot, pressing into tomato mixture.

2. Secure lid and move pressure release valve to sealing or locked position. Cook at high pressure 20 minutes.

3. When cooking is complete, use natural release for 10 minutes, then release remaining pressure. Remove turkey to plate.

4. Press Sauté; cook sauce 10 to 15 minutes or until reduced by one third.

5. Meanwhile, shred turkey into bite-size pieces when cool enough to handle. Add shredded turkey and lemon juice to sauce; mix well. Serve with rice and beans, if desired.

Makes 4 servings

Autumn Chicken and Vegetables

3 to 4 pounds bone-in chicken thighs

½ teaspoon salt

½ teaspoon black pepper

½ cup all-purpose flour

2 tablespoons olive oil

½ cup apple cider or juice

¼ cup chicken broth

1 teaspoon dried thyme

1 small butternut squash, cut into ¾-inch pieces (3 to 4 cups)

1 bulb fennel, thinly sliced

½ cup walnuts (optional)

¼ cup fresh basil leaves, very thinly sliced (optional)

1. Season chicken with salt and pepper; coat lightly with flour. Press Sauté; heat oil in pot. Add chicken in batches; cook about 8 minutes or until browned on both sides. Remove to plate. Stir in cider, broth and thyme; cook 1 minute, scraping up browned bits from bottom of pot. Return chicken to pot, pressing into liquid.

2. Secure lid and move pressure release valve to sealing or locked position. Cook at high pressure 6 minutes.

3. When cooking is complete, press Cancel or Stop and use quick release.

4. Add squash and fennel to pot. Secure lid and move pressure release valve to sealing or locked position. Cook at high pressure 3 minutes.

5. When cooking is complete, press Cancel or Stop and use quick release. Remove chicken and vegetables to platter; cover loosely to keep warm.

6. Press Sauté; cook sauce about 5 minutes or until slightly thickened and reduced by one third. Serve sauce with chicken and vegetables; sprinkle with walnuts and basil, if desired.

Makes 6 servings

Barbecue Turkey Drumsticks

⅓ cup white vinegar

⅓ cup ketchup

⅓ cup molasses

2 tablespoons Worcestershire sauce

2 teaspoons onion powder

2 teaspoons garlic powder

¾ teaspoon liquid smoke

⅛ teaspoon ground chipotle chile pepper

4 turkey drumsticks (8 to 12 ounces each)

1¼ teaspoons salt

1¼ teaspoons black pepper

1. Combine vinegar, ketchup, molasses, Worcestershire sauce, onion powder, garlic powder, liquid smoke and chipotle in measuring cup or medium bowl; mix well.

2. Season drumsticks with salt and pepper; place in pot. Pour sauce over drumsticks, turning to coat completely.

3. Secure lid and move pressure release valve to sealing or locked position. Cook at high pressure 35 minutes.

4. When cooking is complete, use natural release. Remove drumsticks from pot; let stand 10 minutes before serving. Serve with remaining sauce.

Makes 4 servings

Provençal Lemon and Olive Chicken

2 cups chopped onions

2½ pounds bone-in skinless chicken thighs

1 lemon, thinly sliced and seeded

1 cup pitted green olives

1 tablespoon olive brine or white vinegar

2 teaspoons herbes de Provence*

1 bay leaf

1 teaspoon salt

¼ teaspoon black pepper

⅓ cup chicken broth

½ cup minced fresh Italian parsley

Or substitute ½ teaspoon each dried rosemary, thyme, sage and savory.

1. Place onions in pot. Arrange chicken over onions; top with lemon slices. Add olives, brine, herbes de Provence, bay leaf, salt and pepper. Pour in broth.

2. Secure lid and move pressure release valve to sealing or locked position. Cook at high pressure 10 minutes.

3. When cooking is complete, press Cancel or Stop and use quick release. Remove chicken to plate; cover loosely to keep warm.

4. Press Sauté; cook sauce about 5 minutes or until reduced by one third. Remove and discard bay leaf; stir in parsley. Serve sauce with chicken.

Makes 4 servings

Spanish Chicken and Rice

2 tablespoons olive oil

1 package (about 12 ounces) kielbasa sausage, cut into ½-inch slices

2 pounds boneless skinless chicken thighs

1 onion, chopped

4 cloves garlic, minced

2 cups uncooked long grain rice

1 red bell pepper, diced

½ cup diced carrots

¾ teaspoon salt

¼ teaspoon black pepper

¼ teaspoon saffron threads (optional)

3 cups chicken broth

½ cup thawed frozen peas

1. Press Sauté; heat oil in pot. Add sausage; cook about 6 minutes or until browned. Remove to plate. Add chicken to pot in batches; cook about 8 minutes or until browned on all sides. Remove to plate.

2. Add onion to pot; cook and stir 3 minutes or until softened. Add garlic; cook and stir 30 seconds. Add rice, bell pepper, carrots, salt, black pepper and saffron, if desired; cook and stir 3 minutes. Stir in broth, scraping up browned bits from bottom of pot. Return chicken and sausage to pot, pressing chicken into liquid.

3. Secure lid and move pressure release valve to sealing or locked position. Cook at high pressure 7 minutes.

4. When cooking is complete, press Cancel or Stop and use quick release. Remove chicken to clean plate; cover loosely to keep warm.

5. Stir in peas; let stand 2 minutes or until peas are heated through.

Makes 6 servings

Mustard, Garlic and Herb Turkey Breast

1 tablespoon vegetable oil

1 bone-in turkey breast (about 3½ pounds), skin removed

2 tablespoons spicy brown mustard

2 tablespoons chopped fresh parsley

1 tablespoon chopped fresh thyme *or* 1 teaspoon dried thyme

1 tablespoon chopped fresh sage *or* 1 teaspoon dried sage

1 clove garlic, minced

1 teaspoon salt

½ teaspoon black pepper

1½ cups water

¼ cup all-purpose flour (optional)

1. Press Sauté; heat oil in pot. Add turkey; cook about 10 minutes or until browned on all sides.

2. Meanwhile, combine mustard, parsley, thyme, sage, garlic, salt and pepper in small bowl; mix well. Remove turkey from pot; rub herb mixture into all sides of turkey. Pour water into pot. Place rack in pot; place turkey on rack.

3. Secure lid and move pressure release valve to sealing or locked position. Cook at high pressure 30 minutes.

4. When cooking is complete, use natural release for 10 minutes, then release remaining pressure. Remove turkey to cutting board; cover loosely to keep warm. Let stand 10 minutes before slicing.

5. If desired, prepare gravy with cooking liquid. Stir flour into ½ cup cooking liquid in small bowl until smooth. Press Sauté; add flour mixture to pot. Cook about 5 minutes or until gravy is thickened, stirring frequently.

Makes 4 to 6 servings

Basque Chicken with Peppers

1 cut-up whole chicken
(3½ to 4 pounds)*

2 teaspoons salt, divided

1 teaspoon black pepper, divided

1½ tablespoons olive oil

1 onion, chopped

2 red, yellow or green bell peppers
(or a combination), cut into
strips

8 ounces small brown mushrooms,
halved

2 cloves garlic, minced

1 teaspoon smoked paprika

½ teaspoon dried thyme

1 can (about 14 ounces) stewed
tomatoes

2 tablespoons tomato paste

1 tablespoon all-purpose flour
(optional)

2 tablespoons water (optional)

4 ounces chopped prosciutto

*Or purchase 2 leg quarters and 2 breasts
and cut each into two pieces.*

1. Season chicken with 1 teaspoon salt and
½ teaspoon black pepper. Press Sauté; heat oil in
pot. Add chicken in batches; cook about 8 minutes
or until browned on all sides. Remove to plate.

2. Add onion to pot; cook and stir 3 minutes or
until softened. Add bell peppers and mushrooms;
cook and stir 4 minutes or until mushrooms
have released their liquid. Add garlic, smoked
paprika and thyme; cook and stir 1 minute. Stir
in tomatoes, tomato paste, remaining 1 teaspoon
salt and ½ teaspoon black pepper; mix well.
Return chicken to pot, arranging legs and thighs
on bottom and breasts on top. Spoon some of
tomato mixture over chicken.

3. Secure lid and move pressure release valve
to sealing or locked position. Cook at high
pressure 10 minutes.

4. When cooking is complete, press Cancel or
Stop and use quick release. Remove chicken
to clean plate; cover loosely to keep warm.

5. If thicker sauce is desired, stir flour into water in
small bowl until smooth. Press Sauté; add flour
mixture to pot. Cook about 5 minutes or until
sauce is thickened, stirring frequently. Serve
sauce with chicken and vegetables; sprinkle
with prosciutto.

Makes 4 servings

Tuscan Chicken Breasts

Polenta (recipe follows, optional)

6 plum tomatoes, coarsely chopped

½ teaspoon salt, divided

½ teaspoon garlic powder

½ teaspoon Italian seasoning

¾ teaspoon black pepper, divided

6 boneless skinless chicken breasts (about 8 ounces each)

1 tablespoon vegetable oil

½ cup chopped onion

2 cloves garlic, minced

1 can (8 ounces) tomato sauce

2 teaspoons dried basil

2 teaspoons dried oregano

2 teaspoons dried rosemary

1. Prepare and refrigerate Polenta up to a day in advance, if desired.

2. Place tomatoes in colander; toss with ¼ teaspoon salt. Let tomatoes drain while preparing chicken. Combine garlic powder, Italian seasoning, remaining ¼ teaspoon salt and ¼ teaspoon pepper in small bowl; mix well. Rub spice mixture into both sides of chicken.

3. Press Sauté; heat oil in pot. Add chicken in batches; cook about 8 minutes until browned on both sides. Remove to plate.

4. Add onion; cook and stir 3 minutes or until beginning to brown. Add garlic; cook and stir 15 seconds. Stir in drained plum tomatoes, tomato sauce, basil, oregano, rosemary and remaining ½ teaspoon pepper, scraping up browned bits from bottom of pot. Return chicken to pot, pressing into tomato mixture.

5. Secure lid and move pressure release valve to sealing or locked position. Cook at high pressure 6 minutes.

6. When cooking is complete, press Cancel or Stop and use quick release. Remove chicken to clean plate; cover to keep warm. Press Sauté; cook sauce about 10 minutes or until slightly thickened, stirring occasionally. Serve sauce with chicken and polenta, if desired.

Makes 8 servings

Polenta: Bring 4 cups chicken broth to a boil in large saucepan over high heat. Slowly stir in 1 cup polenta (not instant) or yellow cornmeal. Reduce heat to low; cook 15 to 20 minutes or until very thick, stirring frequently. (Mixture may be lumpy.) Pour into greased 9×5-inch loaf pan. Cool to room temperature; cover and refrigerate 2 to 3 hours or until firm. To serve, remove from pan and cut crosswise into 16 slices. Cut slices into triangles, if desired. Spray large nonstick skillet with nonstick cooking spray; cook polenta over medium heat about 4 minutes per side or until lightly browned.

Braised Chicken and Vegetables

¾ cup chicken broth

2 tablespoons lemon juice

2 cloves garlic, minced

1½ teaspoons Italian seasoning

¾ teaspoon cornstarch

½ teaspoon salt

½ teaspoon dried rosemary

½ teaspoon paprika

¼ teaspoon black pepper

4 chicken drumsticks, skin removed

1 yellow squash, cut into ½-inch pieces

1 zucchini, cut into ½-inch pieces

1 onion, cut into ½-inch pieces

1 small red bell pepper, cut into ½-inch pieces

1. Combine broth, lemon juice, garlic, Italian seasoning, cornstarch, salt, rosemary, paprika and black pepper in pot; mix well. Add chicken; stir to coat.

2. Secure lid and move pressure release valve to sealing or locked position. Cook at high pressure 10 minutes.

3. When cooking is complete, press Cancel or Stop and use quick release.

4. Add squash, zucchini, onion and bell pepper to pot; press into cooking liquid. Secure lid and move pressure release valve to sealing or locked position. Cook at high pressure 1 minute.

5. When cooking is complete, press Cancel or Stop and use quick release. Remove chicken and vegetables to platter with slotted spoon; cover loosely to keep warm.

6. Press Sauté; cook sauce about 5 minutes or until slightly reduced. Serve sauce over chicken and vegetables.

Makes 2 to 4 servings

Herb Lemon Turkey Breast

½ cup lemon juice

½ cup dry white wine

4 cloves garlic, minced

1 teaspoon salt

½ teaspoon dried parsley flakes

½ teaspoon dried tarragon

½ teaspoon dried rosemary

¼ teaspoon ground sage

¼ teaspoon black pepper

1 turkey breast (about 3 pounds)

Fresh herbs and lemon slices (optional)

1. Combine lemon juice, wine, garlic, salt, parsley flakes, tarragon, dried rosemary, sage and pepper in measuring cup or small bowl; mix well.

2. Place turkey breast in pot; pour juice mixture over turkey, turning to coat. (Turkey should be right side up for cooking.)

3. Secure lid and move pressure release valve to sealing or locked position. Cook at high pressure 30 minutes.

4. When cooking is complete, use natural release for 10 minutes, then release remaining pressure. Remove turkey to cutting board; cover loosely to keep warm. Let stand 10 minutes before slicing.

5. Use cooking liquid as sauce, if desired, or thicken liquid with flour (see Tip). Garnish as desired.

Makes 4 servings

Tip: If desired, prepare gravy with cooking liquid after removing turkey from pot. Place ¼ cup all-purpose flour in small bowl; stir in ½ cup cooking liquid until smooth. Press Sauté; add flour mixture to pot. Cook 5 minutes or until gravy is thickened, stirring frequently.

Classic Deviled Eggs

1 cup water

6 eggs

Ice water

3 tablespoons mayonnaise

1 tablespoon minced fresh dill *or* 1 teaspoon dried dill weed

1 tablespoon minced dill pickle (optional)

1 teaspoon Dijon mustard

¼ teaspoon salt

⅛ teaspoon white pepper

Paprika (optional)

Fresh dill sprigs (optional)

1. Pour 1 cup water into pot. Place rack in pot; place eggs on rack (or use steamer basket to hold eggs).

2. Secure lid and move pressure release valve to sealing or locked position. Cook at low pressure 9 minutes.

3. When cooking is complete, press Cancel or Stop and use quick release. Immediately transfer eggs to bowl of ice water; let cool 5 to 10 minutes.

4. Peel eggs; cut in half lengthwise. Place yolks to small bowl. Add mayonnaise, dill, pickle, if desired, mustard, salt and pepper; mash with fork until well blended.

5. Fill egg halves with yolk mixture using teaspoon or piping bag fitted with large plain tip. Garnish with paprika and dill sprigs.

Makes 6 servings

Tips: You can use this method to cook 3 to 12 eggs. If you don't need to use the eggs right away, store them unpeeled in the refrigerator for up to 1 week. For soft-boiled eggs, cook at low pressure 3 to 4 minutes. For eggs in between soft and hard-cooked, cook at low pressure 5 to 7 minutes. Remove to a bowl of ice water after cooking as directed above.

SEAFOOD

Miso Salmon

½ cup water

2 green onions, cut into 2-inch pieces

¼ cup yellow miso paste

¼ cup soy sauce

2 tablespoons sake

2 tablespoons mirin

1½ teaspoons grated fresh ginger

1 teaspoon minced garlic

6 salmon fillets (about 4 ounces each)

Hot cooked rice (optional)

Thinly sliced green onions (optional)

1. Combine water, 2 green onions, miso paste, soy sauce, sake, mirin, ginger and garlic in pot; mix well. Add salmon to pot, skin side down.

2. Secure lid and move pressure release valve to sealing or locked position. Cook at low pressure 4 minutes.

3. When cooking is complete, press Cancel or Stop and use quick release. Serve salmon with rice, if desired. Garnish with sliced green onions; drizzle with cooking liquid.

Makes 6 servings

Italian Fish Soup

1 can (about 14 ounces) Italian-seasoned diced tomatoes

1 cup chicken broth

1 small bulb fennel, chopped (about 1 cup), fronds reserved for garnish

3 cloves garlic, minced

1 tablespoon olive oil

½ teaspoon saffron threads, crushed (optional)

½ teaspoon dried basil

¼ teaspoon salt

¼ teaspoon red pepper flakes

8 ounces skinless halibut or cod fillets, cut into 1-inch pieces

8 ounces raw medium shrimp, peeled and deveined

1. Combine tomatoes, broth, chopped fennel, garlic, oil, saffron, if desired, basil, salt and red pepper flakes in pot; mix well.

2. Secure lid and move pressure release valve to sealing or locked position. Cook at high pressure 3 minutes.

3. When cooking is complete, press Cancel or Stop and use quick release.

4. Add halibut to pot. Secure lid and move pressure release valve to sealing or locked position. Cook at low pressure 1 minute.

5. When cooking is complete, press Cancel or Stop and use quick release.

6. Press Sauté. Add shrimp; cook 2 to 3 minutes or until shrimp are pink and opaque, stirring occasionally. Garnish with fennel fronds.

Makes 4 servings

Cod with Tapenade

Tapenade (recipe follows)

4 cod fillets or other firm white fish (about 8 ounces each)

¼ teaspoon salt

⅛ teaspoon black pepper

2 lemons, thinly sliced

1 cup water

1. Prepare Tapenade.

2. Season cod with salt and pepper. Reserve 2 lemon slices for garnish, if desired. Place rack in pot; arrange half of remaining lemon slices on rack. Place cod on lemon slices; top with remaining lemon slices. Pour water into pot.

3. Secure lid and move pressure release valve to sealing or locked position. Cook at low pressure 2 minutes.

4. When cooking is complete, press Cancel or Stop and use quick release. Remove fish to serving plates; discard lemon slices. Serve with Tapenade; garnish with reserved lemon slices.

Makes 4 servings

Tapenade

8 ounces pitted kalamata olives

2 tablespoons anchovy paste

2 tablespoons drained capers

2 tablespoons chopped fresh Italian parsley

1 clove garlic

½ teaspoon grated orange peel

⅛ teaspoon ground red pepper

½ cup extra virgin olive oil

Combine olives, anchovy paste, capers, parsley, garlic, orange peel and red pepper in food processor; pulse until roughly chopped. Add oil; pulse until mixture forms rough paste. (Tapenade should not be completely smooth.)

Makes about 1 cup

New England Fish Chowder

4 slices bacon, chopped

1 cup chopped onion

½ cup chopped celery

2 cups plus 2 tablespoons water, divided

2 cups peeled russet potatoes, cut into 1-inch pieces

1 teaspoon dried dill weed

½ teaspoon dried thyme

½ teaspoon salt

½ teaspoon black pepper

1 bay leaf

1 pound cod, haddock, or halibut fillets, skinned, boned and cut into 1-inch pieces*

2 tablespoons all-purpose flour

2 cups milk or half-and-half

*If fillets are very thin, cut into larger pieces to prevent overcooking.

1. Press Sauté; cook bacon in pot until crisp. Remove to paper towel-lined plate.

2. Add onion and celery to pot; cook and stir 3 minutes or until vegetables are softened. Add 2 cups water, potatoes, dill, thyme, salt, pepper and bay leaf; mix well.

3. Secure lid and move pressure release valve to sealing or locked position. Cook at high pressure 2 minutes.

4. When cooking is complete, press Cancel or Stop and use quick release.

5. Add cod to pot. Secure lid and move pressure release valve to sealing or locked position. Cook at low pressure 1 minute. When cooking is complete, press Cancel or Stop and use quick release.

6. Stir remaining 2 tablespoons water into flour in small bowl until smooth. Press Sauté; adjust heat to low. Add flour mixture to soup; cook and stir 3 minutes or until thickened. Add milk and bacon; cook 2 minutes or until heated through, stirring gently. (Do not boil.) Remove and discard bay leaf.

Makes 4 to 6 servings

Southwestern Salmon Po' Boys

½ teaspoon Southwest seasoning or ground chipotle chile pepper

¼ teaspoon salt

¼ teaspoon black pepper

4 salmon fillets (about 6 ounces each), rinsed and patted dry

1 red bell pepper, thinly sliced

1 green bell pepper, thinly sliced

1 onion, thinly sliced

½ cup Italian dressing

¼ cup water

4 large French sandwich rolls, split *or* French bread, cut into 6-inch pieces and split

¼ cup chipotle mayonnaise*

Fresh cilantro leaves (optional)

½ lemon, cut into 4 wedges

*If unavailable, combine ¼ cup mayonnaise with ½ teaspoon adobo sauce. Or substitute regular mayonnaise.

1. Combine Southwest seasoning, salt and black pepper in small bowl; mix well. Rub spice mixture over both sides of salmon.

2. Combine half of bell peppers and half of onion in pot. Place salmon on top of vegetables. Pour Italian dressing over salmon; top with remaining bell peppers and onion. Pour water into pot.

3. Secure lid and move pressure release valve to sealing or locked position. Cook at low pressure 4 minutes.

4. When cooking is complete, press Cancel or Stop and use quick release. Remove salmon to plate; remove and discard skin.

5. Toast rolls, if desired. Spread top halves with chipotle mayonnaise and cilantro, if desired. Spoon 1 to 2 tablespoons cooking liquid onto bottom halves of rolls; top with warm salmon, vegetable mixture and top halves of rolls. Serve with lemon wedges.

Makes 4 servings

Shrimp and Okra Gumbo

1 tablespoon olive oil

8 ounces kielbasa, halved lengthwise then cut crosswise into ¼-inch slices

1 green bell pepper, chopped

1 medium onion, chopped

3 stalks celery, cut into ¼-inch slices

6 green onions, chopped

4 cloves garlic, minced

1 can (about 14 ounces) diced tomatoes

½ cup chicken broth

1 teaspoon Cajun seasoning

½ teaspoon dried thyme

¼ teaspoon salt

2 cups frozen cut okra, thawed

1 pound large raw shrimp, peeled and deveined (with tails on)

1. Press Sauté; heat oil in pot. Add kielbasa; cook and stir 4 minutes or until browned. Remove to plate.

2. Add bell pepper, chopped onion, celery, green onions and garlic to pot; cook and stir 6 minutes or until vegetables are softened. Stir in tomatoes, broth, Cajun seasoning, thyme and salt; mix well.

3. Secure lid and move pressure release valve to sealing or locked position. Cook at high pressure 4 minutes.

4. When cooking is complete, press Cancel or Stop and use quick release.

5. Add okra to pot. Secure lid and move pressure release valve to sealing or locked position. Cook at high pressure 1 minute. When cooking is complete, press Cancel or Stop and use quick release.

6. Press Sauté; stir in shrimp. Cook 2 to 3 minutes or until shrimp are pink and opaque, stirring occasionally.

Makes 6 servings

Sea Bass with Vegetables

2 tablespoons butter or olive oil

2 bulbs fennel, thinly sliced

3 large carrots, julienned

3 large leeks, thinly sliced

¾ teaspoon salt, divided

¼ teaspoon plus ⅛ teaspoon black pepper, divided

6 sea bass fillets or other firm-fleshed white fish (6 to 8 ounces each)

¼ cup water

1. Press Sauté; melt butter in pot. Add fennel, carrots and leeks; cook about 8 minutes or until vegetables are softened and beginning to brown, stirring occasionally. Stir in ½ teaspoon salt and ¼ teaspoon pepper. Remove half of vegetables to plate.

2. Season sea bass with remaining ¼ teaspoon salt and ⅛ teaspoon pepper; place on top of vegetables in pot. Top with reserved vegetables. Drizzle with water.

3. Secure lid and move pressure release valve to sealing or locked position. Cook at low pressure 4 minutes.

4. When cooking is complete, press Cancel or Stop and use quick release. Serve sea bass with vegetables.

Makes 6 servings

Savory Cod Stew

8 ounces bacon, chopped

1 large onion, diced

1 large carrot, diced

2 stalks celery, diced

2 cloves garlic, minced

1 can (28 ounces) plum tomatoes, undrained, coarsely chopped

2 potatoes, peeled and diced

1 cup clam juice

3 tablespoons tomato paste

3 tablespoons chopped fresh Italian parsley

½ teaspoon salt

¼ teaspoon black pepper

3 saffron threads

2½ pounds fresh cod, skin removed, cut into 1½-inch pieces

1. Press Sauté; cook bacon in pot until crisp. Drain off all but 2 tablespoons drippings.

2. Add onion, carrot, celery and garlic to pot; cook and stir 5 minutes or until vegetables are softened. Add tomatoes with liquid, potatoes, clam juice, tomato paste, parsley, salt, pepper and saffron; cook and stir 2 minutes.

3. Secure lid and move pressure release valve to sealing or locked position. Cook at high pressure 2 minutes.

4. When cooking is complete, press Cancel or Stop and use quick release.

5. Add cod to pot. Secure lid and move pressure release valve to sealing or locked position. Cook at low pressure 1 minute.

6. When cooking is complete, press Cancel or Stop and use quick release.

Makes 6 to 8 servings

BEANS & GRAINS

Southwestern Corn and Beans

2 cup dried kidney beans, soaked 8 hours or overnight

1 tablespoon olive oil

1 large onion, chopped

1 jalapeño pepper, minced*

1 clove garlic, minced

2 teaspoons chili powder

½ teaspoon ground cumin

1 can (about 14 ounces) diced tomatoes

1 green bell pepper, cut into 1-inch pieces

½ cup water

1½ teaspoons salt

½ teaspoon black pepper

1 package (16 ounces) frozen corn, thawed

Tortilla chips, sour cream and sliced black olives (optional)

*Jalapeño peppers can sting and irritate the skin, so wear rubber gloves when handling peppers and do not touch your eyes.

1. Drain and rinse beans. Press Sauté; heat oil in pot. Add onion; cook and stir 3 minutes or until softened. Add jalapeño, garlic, chili powder and cumin; cook and stir 1 minute. Add tomatoes, bell pepper, water, salt and black pepper; mix well. Stir in beans.

2. Secure lid and move pressure release valve to sealing or locked position. Cook at high pressure 25 minutes.

3. When cooking is complete, use natural release for 10 minutes, then release remaining pressure.

4. Press Sauté; stir in corn. Cook about 5 minutes or until mixture has thickened and corn is heated through, stirring occasionally. Serve with tortilla chips, sour cream and olives, if desired.

Makes 6 servings

Farro Risotto with Mushrooms and Spinach

2 tablespoons olive oil, divided

1 onion, chopped

12 ounces cremini mushrooms, stems trimmed, quartered

1 teaspoon salt

¼ teaspoon black pepper

2 cloves garlic, minced

1 cup uncooked pearled farro

1 sprig fresh thyme

1½ cups vegetable or chicken broth

1 package (5 to 6 ounces) baby spinach

½ cup grated Parmesan cheese

1. Press Sauté; heat 1 tablespoon oil in pot. Add onion; cook and stir 5 minutes or until translucent. Add remaining 1 tablespoon oil, mushrooms, salt and pepper; cook about 8 minutes or until mushrooms have released their liquid and are browned. Add garlic; cook and stir 1 minute. Stir in farro and thyme; cook 1 minute. Add broth; mix well.

2. Secure lid and move pressure release valve to sealing or locked position. Cook at high pressure 10 minutes.

3. When cooking is complete, use natural release for 10 minutes, then release remaining pressure. Remove and discard thyme sprig.

4. Stir in spinach and cheese until spinach is wilted.

Makes 4 servings

Classic Irish Oatmeal

2 tablespoons butter

1 cup steel-cut oats

3 cups water

½ teaspoon salt

½ teaspoon ground cinnamon

Berry Compote
(recipe follows, optional)

⅓ cup half-and-half

¼ cup packed brown sugar

1. Press Sauté; melt butter in pot. Add oats; cook about 5 minutes, stirring frequently. Add water, salt and cinnamon; cook and stir 1 minute.

2. Secure lid and move pressure release valve to sealing or locked position. Cook at high pressure 13 minutes.

3. Meanwhile, prepare Berry Compote, if desired.

4. When cooking is complete, press Cancel or Stop to turn off heat. Use natural release for 10 minutes, then release remaining pressure.

5. Stir oats until smooth. Add half-and-half and brown sugar; stir until well blended. If thicker oatmeal is desired, press Sauté and cook 2 to 3 minutes or until desired thickness, stirring constantly. (Oatmeal will also thicken upon standing.) Serve with Berry Compote.

Makes 4 servings

Berry Compote: Combine 1 cup quartered fresh strawberries, 6 ounces fresh blackberries, 6 ounces fresh blueberries, 3 tablespoons granulated sugar and 1 tablespoon water in medium saucepan; bring to a simmer over medium heat. Cook 8 to 9 minutes or until berries are tender but still hold their shape, stirring occasionally.

Black Bean Chili

1 pound dried black beans,
   soaked 8 hours or overnight

1 tablespoon olive oil

1 large onion, chopped

1 large jalapeño pepper,* minced

3 cloves garlic, minced

2 tablespoons chili powder

2 teaspoons salt

1 teaspoon paprika

1 teaspoon dried oregano

1 teaspoon unsweetened
   cocoa powder

½ teaspoon ground cumin

¼ teaspoon ground cinnamon

2 cups water

1 can (about 14 ounces) diced
   tomatoes

1 bay leaf

1 to 2 tablespoons lime juice

   Plain yogurt or sour cream,
   picante sauce, sliced green
   onions, chopped fresh cilantro
   (optional)

*Jalapeño peppers can sting and irritate the skin,
so wear rubber gloves when handling peppers
and do not touch your eyes.

1. Drain and rinse beans. Press Sauté; heat oil in pot. Add onion; cook and stir 5 minutes. Add jalapeño, garlic, chili powder, salt, paprika, oregano, cocoa, cumin and cinnamon; cook and stir 1 minute. Add beans, water, tomatoes and bay leaf; mix well.

2. Secure lid and move pressure release valve to sealing or locked position. Cook at high pressure 8 minutes.

3. When cooking is complete, use natural release for 15 minutes, then release remaining pressure.

4. For thicker chili, press Sauté and cook 3 to 5 minutes or until thickened, stirring frequently. (Chili will also thicken upon standing.) Remove and discard bay leaf. Stir in lime juice; serve with desired toppings.

Makes 6 servings

Tip: For a heartier meal, hollow out small loaves of sourdough or crusty Italian bread and serve the chili in bread bowls.

Cheesy Polenta

5 cups vegetable broth

½ teaspoon salt

1½ cups uncooked instant polenta

½ cup grated Parmesan cheese, plus additional for serving

4 tablespoons (½ stick) butter, cubed

Fried sage leaves (optional)

1. Combine broth and salt in pot; slowly whisk in polenta until blended.

2. Secure lid and move pressure release valve to sealing or locked position. Cook at high pressure 5 minutes.

3. When cooking is complete, use natural release for 5 minutes, then release remaining pressure.

4. Whisk in ½ cup cheese and butter until well blended. (Polenta may appear separated immediately after cooking but will come together when stirred.) Serve with additional cheese; garnish with sage.

Makes 6 servings

Tip: Spread any leftover polenta in a baking dish and refrigerate until cold. Cut the cold polenta into sticks or slices, brush with olive oil and pan-fry or grill until lightly browned.

Note: Chicken broth may be substituted for vegetable broth. Or use water and add an additional ½ teaspoon salt when whisking in the polenta.

Winter Squash Risotto

2 tablespoons butter

1 tablespoon olive oil

1 large shallot or small onion, finely chopped

1½ cups uncooked arborio rice

1 teaspoon salt

½ teaspoon dried thyme

¼ teaspoon black pepper

¼ cup dry white wine

4 cups vegetable or chicken broth

2 cups cubed butternut squash (½-inch pieces)

½ grated Parmesan or Romano cheese, plus additional for garnish

1. Press Sauté; heat butter and oil in pot. Add shallot; cook and stir 2 minutes or until softened. Add rice; cook and stir 4 minutes or until rice is translucent. Stir in salt, thyme and pepper. Add wine; cook and stir about 1 minute or until evaporated. Add broth and squash; mix well.

2. Secure lid and move pressure release valve to sealing or locked position. Cook at high pressure 6 minutes.

3. When cooking is complete, press Cancel or Stop and use quick release.

4. Press Sauté; adjust heat to low. Cook risotto about 3 minutes or until desired consistency, stirring constantly. Stir in ½ cup cheese. Serve immediately with additional cheese.

Makes 4 to 6 servings

Quinoa and Mango Salad

1 cup uncooked quinoa

1½ cups water

¾ teaspoon salt, divided

2 cups cubed peeled mangoes (about 2 large mangoes)

½ cup sliced green onions

½ cup dried cranberries

2 tablespoons chopped fresh parsley

¼ cup extra virgin olive oil

1½ tablespoons white wine vinegar

1 teaspoon Dijon mustard

⅛ teaspoon black pepper

1. Place quinoa in fine-mesh strainer; rinse under cold running water and drain. Combine quinoa, 1½ cups water and ¼ teaspoon salt in pot; mix well.

2. Secure lid and move pressure release valve to sealing or locked position. Cook at high pressure 1 minute.

3. When cooking is complete, use natural release for 10 minutes, then release remaining pressure.

4. If any liquid remains in pot, press Sauté; cook and stir 1 minute or until liquid has evaporated. Spread quinoa on large plate or in baking dish; cover loosely and refrigerate at least 30 minutes.

5. Add mangoes, green onions, cranberries and parsley to quinoa; mix well. Combine oil, vinegar, mustard, remaining ½ teaspoon salt and pepper in small bowl; whisk until blended. Pour over quinoa mixture; stir until well blended.

Makes 6 servings

Tip: This salad can be made several hours ahead and refrigerated. Let stand at room temperature for at least 30 minutes before serving.

Easy Herbed Rice

1½ cups uncooked long grain rice

1½ cups water

2 tablespoons minced onion

2 tablespoons butter

1 clove garlic, minced

½ teaspoon salt

2 tablespoons minced fresh parsley

2 tablespoons minced fresh basil *or* 1 teaspoon dried basil*

2 tablespoons minced fresh oregano *or* 1 teaspoon dried oregano*

If using dried herbs, add to rice before cooking.

1. Rinse rice well; drain in fine-mesh strainer. Combine rice, water, onion, butter, garlic and salt in pot; mix well.

2. Secure lid and move pressure release valve to sealing or locked position. Cook at high pressure 4 minutes.

3. When cooking is complete, use natural release for 10 minutes, then release remaining pressure.

4. Stir in parsley, basil and oregano. Fluff rice gently with fork.

Makes 4 to 6 servings

Tip: To make this recipe with brown rice, cook at high pressure 22 minutes.

BBQ "Baked" Beans

4 slices bacon, chopped

1 onion, chopped

2 cloves garlic, minced

1 package (16 ounces) dried Great Northern beans, soaked 8 hours or overnight

1 can (about 14 ounces) diced tomatoes

1 cup water

¼ cup ketchup

3 tablespoons maple syrup

3 tablespoons molasses

2 tablespoons packed brown sugar

¾ teaspoon salt

½ teaspoon dry mustard

⅛ teaspoon black pepper

1. Drain and rinse beans. Press Sauté; cook bacon in pot until crisp.

2. Add onion; cook and stir 3 minutes or until softened. Add garlic; cook and stir 1 minute. Stir in beans, tomatoes, water, ketchup, maple syrup, molasses, brown sugar, salt, mustard and pepper; mix well.

3. Secure lid and move pressure release valve to sealing or locked position. Cook at high pressure 45 minutes.

4. When cooking is complete, use natural release for 10 minutes, then release remaining pressure.

Makes 4 to 6 servings

Variation: For a vegetarian version, omit the bacon. Sauté the onion and garlic in 1 tablespoon olive oil in step 1, then proceed as directed above.

Superfood Breakfast Porridge

¾ cup steel-cut oats

¼ cup uncooked quinoa, rinsed and drained

¼ cup dried cranberries, plus additional for serving

¼ cup raisins

3 tablespoons ground flax seeds

2 tablespoons chia seeds

1 teaspoon olive oil

¼ teaspoon salt

¼ teaspoon ground cinnamon

2½ cups almond milk, plus additional for serving

1½ cups water

Maple syrup (optional)

¼ cup sliced almonds, toasted* (optional)

To toast almonds, cook and stir in small skillet over medium heat 2 to 3 minutes or until nuts are lightly browned.

1. Spray heatproof bowl (metal, glass or ceramic) that fits inside of pot with nonstick cooking spray. Combine oats, quinoa, ¼ cup cranberries, raisins, flax seeds, chia seeds, oil, salt and cinnamon in prepared bowl; mix well. Stir in 2½ cups almond milk until blended.

2. Pour water into pot. Place rack in pot; place bowl on rack. Secure lid and move pressure release valve to sealing or locked position. Cook at high pressure 13 minutes.

3. When cooking is complete, use natural release.

4. Stir porridge until smooth. Serve with additional almond milk, cranberries, maple syrup and almonds, if desired.

Makes 4 servings

Pesto Rice and Beans

½ cup dried Great Northern beans, soaked 8 hours or overnight

1½ cups water or chicken broth, divided

¼ teaspoon salt, divided

½ cup uncooked long grain rice

4 ounces fresh green beans, cut into 1-inch pieces (about ¾ cup)

¼ cup prepared pesto

Shredded or grated Parmesan cheese, chopped plum tomatoes and chopped fresh parsley (optional)

1. Drain and rinse dried beans. Combine beans, 1 cup water and ⅛ teaspoon salt in pot; mix well. Secure lid and move pressure release valve to sealing or locked position. Cook at high pressure 4 minutes.

2. Meanwhile, rinse rice well; drain in fine-mesh strainer. Combine rice, remaining ½ cup water and ⅛ teaspoon salt in small metal or ceramic bowl that fits inside pot; mix well. Place green beans in center of 12-inch square of foil; sprinkle with additional salt. Bring up two sides of foil over beans; fold foil over several times to create packet. Fold in opposite ends. (Packet should measure about 8×4 inches.)

3. When cooking is complete, press Cancel or Stop and use quick release. Place rack in pot; place bowl with rice on rack. Arrange foil packet on top of bowl. (Packet should not entirely cover bowl.) Secure lid and move pressure release valve to sealing or locked position. Cook at high pressure 4 minutes.

4. When cooking is complete, use natural release for 8 minutes, then release remaining pressure. Remove bowl and foil packet from pot. If any liquid remains in bottom of pot with Great Northern beans, press Sauté; cook 1 to 2 minutes or until liquid is evaporated.

5. Add Great Northern beans and green beans to bowl with rice; gently stir in pesto. Top with cheese, tomatoes and parsley, if desired.

Makes 4 servings

Barley and Vegetable Risotto

1 tablespoon olive oil

1 onion, chopped

1 cup uncooked pearl barley

2 cloves garlic, minced

1½ cups vegetable broth

8 ounces sliced mushrooms

1 large red bell pepper, diced

1 teaspoon salt

2 cups packed baby spinach

½ cup grated Parmesan cheese

¼ teaspoon black pepper

1. Press Sauté; heat oil in pot. Add onion; cook and stir 3 minutes or until softened. Add barley and garlic; cook and stir 1 minute. Stir in broth, mushrooms, bell pepper and salt; mix well.

2. Secure lid and move pressure release valve to sealing or locked position. Cook at high pressure 18 minutes.

3. When cooking is complete, use natural release for 10 minutes, then release remaining pressure.

4. Stir in spinach; let stand 2 to 3 minutes or until spinach is wilted. Gently stir in cheese and black pepper.

Makes 4 to 6 servings

Cheese Grits with Chiles and Bacon

6 slices bacon, chopped

1 large shallot or small onion, finely chopped

1 serrano or jalapeño pepper,* minced

3½ cups chicken broth

1 cup uncooked grits**

½ teaspoon salt

¼ teaspoon black pepper

1 cup (4 ounces) shredded Cheddar cheese

½ cup half-and-half

2 tablespoons finely chopped green onion

*Chile peppers can sting and irritate the skin, so wear rubber gloves when handling peppers and do not touch your eyes.

**Do not use instant grits.

1. Press Sauté; cook bacon in pot until crisp. Drain on paper towel-lined plate. Drain off all but 1 tablespoon drippings.

2. Add shallot and serrano pepper to pot; cook and stir 2 minutes or until shallot is lightly browned. Add broth, grits, salt and black pepper; cook and stir 1 minute.

3. Secure lid and move pressure release valve to sealing or locked position. Cook at high pressure 14 minutes.

4. When cooking is complete, use natural release for 10 minutes, then release remaining pressure.

5. Stir grits until smooth. Add cheese, half-and-half and half of bacon; stir until well blended. Sprinkle with green onion and remaining bacon.

Makes 4 servings

Greek Rice

1¾ cups uncooked long grain rice

2 tablespoons butter

1¾ cups vegetable or chicken broth

1 teaspoon Greek seasoning

1 teaspoon dried oregano

¼ teaspoon salt

1 cup pitted kalamata olives, drained and chopped

¾ cup chopped roasted red peppers

Crumbled feta cheese (optional)

Chopped fresh Italian parsley (optional)

1. Rinse rice well; drain in fine-mesh strainer.

2. Press Sauté; melt butter in pot. Add rice; cook 5 to 6 minutes or until golden brown, stirring occasionally. Add broth, Greek seasoning, oregano and salt; mix well.

3. Secure lid and move pressure release valve to sealing or locked position. Cook at high pressure 4 minutes.

4. When cooking is complete, use natural release for 10 minutes, then release remaining pressure.

5. Stir in olives and roasted red peppers; garnish with cheese and parsley.

Makes 6 to 8 servings

Four-Bean Chili Stew

¾ cup dried kidney beans

¾ cup dried chickpeas

¾ cup dried Great Northern beans

¾ cup dried black beans

2 cans (about 11 ounces each) tomatillos, drained

1 can (about 15 ounces) tomato sauce

1½ cups water

1 cup prepared barbecue sauce

1 onion, chopped

3 cloves garlic, minced

1½ teaspoons ground cumin

1½ teaspoons chili powder

½ teaspoon salt

¼ teaspoon ground red pepper

1 zucchini, cut in half then cut into 1-inch slices

½ red bell pepper, chopped

Flour tortillas, warmed (optional)

Sour cream, chopped tomato, chopped onion, shredded Cheddar cheese and/or chopped fresh cilantro (optional)

1. Rinse beans separately in colander under cold running water, picking out any debris or blemished beans. Combine kidney beans, chickpeas and Great Northern beans in large bowl; cover with water. Place black beans in medium bowl; cover with water.* Soak 8 hours or overnight.

2. Drain and rinse all beans. Place in pot with tomatillos, tomato sauce, 1½ cups water, barbecue sauce, onion, garlic, cumin, chili powder, salt and ground red pepper; mix well.

3. Secure lid and move pressure release valve to sealing or locked position. Cook at high pressure 20 minutes.

4. When cooking is complete, use natural release for 5 minutes, then release remaining pressure.

5. Stir in zucchini and bell pepper. Secure lid and move pressure release valve to sealing or locked position. Cook at high pressure 1 minute.

6. When cooking is complete, press Cancel or Stop and use quick release. Serve with tortillas and desired toppings.

Soaking black beans with the other beans will turn the Great Northerns and chickpeas purple.

Makes 6 servings

Paella Salad

1 cup uncooked brown rice

1 cup chicken broth

¼ teaspoon salt

¼ teaspoon ground turmeric

1 jar (6 ounces) marinated artichokes, drained and marinade liquid reserved

1 tablespoon minced onion

¼ teaspoon dried oregano

1 cup small peeled cooked shrimp (with tails on)

½ cup thawed frozen peas

2 ounces pepperoni, cut into thin julienne strips

1 jar (2 ounces) diced pimientos, drained

Black pepper

1. Rinse rice well; drain in fine-mesh strainer. Combine rice, broth, ¼ teaspoon salt and turmeric in pot; mix well.

2. Secure lid and move pressure release valve to sealing or locked position. Cook at high pressure 22 minutes.

3. When cooking is complete, use natural release for 10 minutes, then release remaining pressure.

4. Transfer rice to large bowl; stir in reserved artichoke marinade, onion and oregano. Fluff rice with fork. Refrigerate 20 minutes or until cool.

5. Add artichokes, shrimp, peas, pepperoni and pimientos to rice mixture; stir gently until blended. Season with additional salt and pepper.

Makes 4 servings

Channna Chat (Indian-Spiced Snack Mix)

1 cup dried chickpeas, soaked 8 hours or overnight

2 teaspoons canola oil

1 medium onion, finely chopped, divided

2 cloves garlic, minced

2 cups vegetable broth or water

1 tablespoon tomato paste

1 teaspoon salt

½ teaspoon ground cinnamon

½ teaspoon ground cumin

¼ teaspoon black pepper

1 bay leaf

½ cup balsamic vinegar

1 tablespoon packed brown sugar

1 plum tomato, chopped

½ jalapeño pepper, minced* or ¼ teaspoon ground red pepper (optional)

½ cup crisp rice cereal

3 tablespoons chopped fresh cilantro (optional)

Jalapeño peppers can sting and irritate the skin, so wear rubber gloves when handling peppers and do not touch your eyes.

1. Drain and rinse beans. Press Sauté; heat oil in pot. Add half of onion and garlic; cook and stir 2 minutes or until softened. Stir in chickpeas, broth, tomato paste, salt, cinnamon, cumin, black pepper and bay leaf; mix well.

2. Secure lid and move pressure release valve to sealing or locked position. Cook at high pressure 15 minutes.

3. When cooking is complete, use natural release for 10 minutes, then release remaining pressure. Remove lid; let chickpeas cool in liquid 15 minutes.

4. Meanwhile, combine balsamic vinegar and brown sugar in small saucepan; cook over medium-low heat 5 minutes or until mixture reduces and becomes syrupy.

5. Drain off and discard 1 cup liquid from chickpeas; remove and discard bay leaf. Toss chickpeas with tomato, remaining onion and jalapeño, if desired. Fold in rice cereal; drizzle with balsamic syrup. Garnish with cilantro.

Makes 6 to 8 servings

Bulgur Pilaf with Caramelized Onions and Kale

1 tablespoon olive oil

1 small onion, cut into thin wedges

1 clove garlic, minced

2 cups chopped kale

2¾ cups vegetable or chicken broth

1 cup medium grain bulgur

1 teaspoon salt

¼ teaspoon black pepper

1. Press Sauté; heat oil in pot. Add onion; cook about 10 minutes or until golden brown, stirring frequently. Add garlic; cook and stir 1 minute. Add kale; cook and stir about 1 minute or until kale is wilted. Stir in broth, bulgur, salt and pepper; mix well.

2. Secure lid and move pressure release valve to sealing or locked position. Cook at high pressure 8 minutes.

3. When cooking is complete, use natural release for 5 minutes, then release remaining pressure.

Makes 4 servings

Risotto with Mushrooms and Sun-Dried Tomatoes

1 tablespoon olive oil

1 tablespoon butter

½ cup minced shallot or onion

1½ cups uncooked arborio rice

¼ cup dry white wine or sherry

½ teaspoon salt

4 cups vegetable or chicken broth

½ cup chopped dried mushrooms

¼ cup chopped sun-dried tomatoes (not packed in oil)

½ cup shredded Parmesan cheese

2 tablespoons pine nuts

1. Press Sauté; heat oil and butter in pot. Add shallot; cook and stir 2 minutes or until softened. Add rice; cook and stir 2 minutes or until translucent. Add wine and salt; cook and stir 1 minute or until wine is absorbed. Stir in broth, mushrooms and tomatoes; mix well.

2. Secure lid and move pressure release valve to sealing or locked position. Cook at high pressure 6 minutes.

3. When cooking is complete, press Cancel or Stop and use quick release.

4. If there is excess liquid in pot, press Sauté and cook 1 minute, stirring constantly. Stir in cheese and pine nuts.

Makes 6 servings

VEGETABLES

Mashed Root Vegetables

1 pound baking potatoes, peeled and cut into 1-inch pieces

1 pound turnips, peeled and cut into 1-inch pieces

12 ounces sweet potatoes, peeled and cut into 1-inch pieces

8 ounces parsnips, peeled and cut into ½-inch pieces

¼ cup (½ stick) butter, cubed

⅓ cup water

2 teaspoons salt

¼ teaspoon black pepper

½ cup milk

1. Combine baking potatoes, turnips, sweet potatoes, parsnips, butter, water, salt and pepper in pot; mix well.

2. Secure lid and move pressure release valve to sealing or locked position. Cook at high pressure 10 minutes.

3. When cooking is complete, press Cancel or Stop and use quick release.

4. Mash vegetables with potato masher until almost smooth. Press Sauté; stir in milk until blended. Cook and stir about 3 minutes or until milk is absorbed and vegetables reach desired consistency.

Makes 6 servings

Cider Vinaigrette-Glazed Beets

6 medium red and/or golden beets
  (about 3 pounds)

1 cup water

2 tablespoons cider vinegar

1 tablespoon extra virgin olive oil

1 teaspoon Dijon mustard

½ teaspoon packed brown sugar

¾ teaspoon salt

¼ teaspoon black pepper

⅓ cup crumbled blue cheese
  (optional)

1. Cut tops off beets, leaving at least 1 inch of stems. Scrub beets under cold running water with soft vegetable brush, being careful not to break skins. Pour 1 cup water into pot. Place rack in pot; place beets on rack (or use steamer basket to hold beets).

2. Secure lid and move pressure release valve to sealing or locked position. Cook at high pressure 22 minutes.

3. When cooking is complete, use natural release for 10 minutes, then release remaining pressure. Check doneness by inserting paring knife into beets; knife should go in easily. If not, cook an additional 2 to 4 minutes.

4. Whisk vinegar, oil, mustard, brown sugar, salt and pepper in medium bowl until well blended.

5. When beets are cool enough to handle, peel off skins and trim root ends. Cut into wedges. Add warm beets to vinaigrette; toss gently to coat. Sprinkle with cheese, if desired. Serve warm or at room temperature.

Makes 6 servings

Tip: The cooking time depends on the size of the beets, which can vary slightly. If beets are not tender enough, close cover and cook under pressure 2 or 4 minutes longer.

Spicy Asian Green Beans

1 cup water

1 pound fresh green beans, trimmed

2 tablespoons chopped green onions

2 tablespoons dry sherry or chicken broth

1½ tablespoons reduced-sodium soy sauce

1 teaspoon chili sauce with garlic

1 teaspoon dark sesame oil

1 clove garlic, minced

1. Pour water into pot. Place rack in pot; place beans on rack. (Arrange beans perpendicular to rack to prevent beans from falling through.)

2. Secure lid and move pressure release valve to sealing or locked position. Cook at high pressure 2 minutes.

3. When cooking is complete, press Cancel or Stop and use quick release. Remove rack from pot; drain off and discard cooking liquid. Place beans in large bowl.

4. Press Sauté; add green onions, sherry, soy sauce, chili sauce, oil and garlic to pot. Cook and stir 1 to 2 minutes or until heated through.

5. Pour sauce over beans; toss to coat.

Makes 4 servings

Quick Vegetable Curry

2 teaspoons salt

2 teaspoons curry powder

1 teaspoon cumin seeds

1 teaspoon ground coriander

¼ teaspoon ground turmeric

¼ teaspoon ground red pepper

1 tablespoon vegetable oil

1 large onion, finely chopped

4 cloves garlic, minced

1 tablespoon grated fresh ginger

¼ cup tomato paste

1 cup water

1 head cauliflower (about 1 pound), broken into florets

2 baking potatoes, peeled and cut into ½-inch pieces

1 red bell pepper, cut into ½-inch pieces

2 carrots, cut into ¼-inch pieces

1 package (12 ounces) frozen peas, thawed

1. Combine salt, curry powder, cumin, coriander, turmeric and ground red pepper in small bowl; mix well.

2. Press Sauté; heat oil in pot. Add onion; cook and stir 3 minutes or until softened. Add garlic, ginger and spice mixture; cook and stir 1 minute. Add tomato paste; cook 30 seconds. Stir in water, scraping up browned bits from bottom of pot. Add cauliflower, potatoes, bell pepper and carrots; stir to coat with sauce.

3. Secure lid and move pressure release valve to sealing or locked position. Cook at high pressure 2 minutes.

4. When cooking is complete, press Cancel or Stop and use quick release.

5. Stir in peas; let stand 2 to 3 minutes or until heated through.

Makes 6 to 8 servings

Sweet and Sour Red Cabbage

2 thick slices bacon, chopped

1 cup chopped onion

1 head red cabbage (2 to 3 pounds), thinly sliced (about 8 cups)

1 pound unpeeled Granny Smith apples, cut into ½-inch pieces (about 2 medium)

½ cup honey

½ cup cider vinegar

¼ cup plus 3 tablespoons water, divided

1 teaspoon salt

1 teaspoon celery salt

¼ teaspoon black pepper

2 tablespoons all-purpose flour

1. Press Sauté, cook and stir bacon in pot until crisp. Remove to paper towel-lined plate.

2. Add onion to pot; cook and stir 3 minutes or until softened. Stir in cabbage, apples, honey, vinegar, ¼ cup water, salt, celery salt and pepper; mix well.

3. Secure lid and move pressure release valve to sealing or locked position. Cook at high pressure 5 minutes.

4. When cooking is complete, use natural release for 10 minutes, then release remaining pressure.

5. Stir remaining 3 tablespoons water into flour in small bowl until smooth. Press Sauté; add flour mixture to pot. Cook and stir about 3 minutes or until thickened. Sprinkle with bacon; serve warm.

Makes 8 servings

Spiced Sweet Potatoes

2½ pounds sweet potatoes, peeled and cut into ½-inch pieces

½ cup water

2 tablespoons dark brown sugar

1 teaspoon salt

1 teaspoon ground cinnamon

½ teaspoon ground nutmeg

2 tablespoons butter, cut into small pieces

½ teaspoon vanilla

1. Combine sweet potatoes, water, brown sugar, salt, cinnamon and nutmeg in pot; mix well.

2. Secure lid and move pressure release valve to sealing or locked position. Cook at high pressure 3 minutes.

3. When cooking is complete, press Cancel or Stop and use quick release.

4. Press Sauté; add butter and vanilla. Cook 1 to 2 minutes or until butter is melted, stirring gently to blend.

Makes 4 to 6 servings

Lemon Parmesan Cauliflower

1 cup water

3 tablespoons chopped fresh parsley

½ teaspoon grated lemon peel

1 large head cauliflower (2 to 3 pounds), trimmed

1 tablespoon butter

3 cloves garlic, minced

2 tablespoons lemon juice

½ teaspoon salt

¼ cup grated Parmesan cheese

1. Pour water into pot; stir in parsley and lemon peel. Place rack in pot; place cauliflower on rack.

2. Secure lid and move pressure release valve to sealing or locked position. Cook at high pressure 3 minutes.

3. When cooking is complete, press Cancel or Stop and use quick release. Remove rack from pot; place cauliflower in large bowl. Reserve ½ cup cooking liquid; drain off and discard remaining liquid.

4. Press Sauté; heat butter in pot. Add garlic; cook and stir 1 minute or until fragrant. Stir in lemon juice, salt and reserved ½ cup cooking liquid; cook and stir until heated through.

5. Spoon lemon sauce over cauliflower; sprinkle with cheese. Cut into wedges to serve.

Makes 6 servings

Fennel Braised with Tomato

2 bulbs fennel

1 tablespoon olive oil

1 small onion, sliced

1 clove garlic, minced

3 tablespoons dry white wine

4 medium tomatoes, chopped

⅓ cup vegetable broth or water

1 tablespoon chopped fresh marjoram *or* 1 teaspoon dried marjoram

½ teaspoon salt

¼ teaspoon black pepper

1. Trim stems and bottoms from fennel bulbs, reserving fronds for garnish. Cut each bulb lengthwise into 4 wedges.

2. Press Sauté; heat oil in pot. Add fennel, onion and garlic; cook and stir 5 minutes or until onion is translucent. Add wine; cook and stir until almost evaporated. Stir in tomatoes, broth, marjoram, salt and pepper; mix well.

3. Secure lid and move pressure release valve to sealing or locked position. Cook at high pressure 4 minutes.

4. When cooking is complete, use natural release for 10 minutes, then release remaining pressure. Transfer vegetables to medium bowl with slotted spoon.

5. Press Sauté; cook liquid remaining in pot about 5 minutes or until reduced by one third. Add to vegetables; mix well. Garnish with reserved fennel fronds.

Makes 6 servings

Coconut Butternut Squash

1 tablespoon butter

½ cup chopped onion

1 butternut squash (about
3 pounds), peeled and
cut into 1-inch pieces

1 can (about 13 ounces) coconut
milk*

1 to 2 tablespoons packed
brown sugar, divided

1¼ teaspoons salt

½ teaspoon ground cinnamon

¼ teaspoon ground nutmeg

¼ teaspoon ground allspice

2 teaspoons grated fresh ginger

2 tablespoons lemon juice

*Shake vigorously before opening to mix
thoroughly.*

1. Press Sauté; melt butter in pot. Add onion;
cook and stir 2 minutes. Add squash, coconut
milk, 1 tablespoon brown sugar, salt, cinnamon,
nutmeg and allspice; mix well.

2. Secure lid and move pressure release valve
to sealing or locked position. Cook at high
pressure 6 minutes.

3. When cooking is complete, press Cancel or
Stop and use quick release.

4. Stir ginger into squash mixture. Use immersion
blender to blend squash until smooth (or process
in food processor or blender). Stir in lemon juice.
Sprinkle individual servings with remaining
1 tablespoon brown sugar, if desired.

Makes 4 to 6 servings

Brussels Sprouts in Orange Sauce

½ cup plus 2 tablespoons orange juice, divided

½ teaspoon salt

¼ teaspoon red pepper flakes

¼ teaspoon ground cinnamon

¼ teaspoon black pepper

8 ounces fresh brussels sprouts, trimmed (about 3 cups)

2 teaspoons cornstarch

1 teaspoon honey

1 teaspoon shredded or grated orange peel

1. Combine ½ cup orange juice, salt, red pepper flakes, cinnamon and black pepper in pot; mix well. Stir in brussels sprouts.

2. Secure lid and move pressure release valve to sealing or locked position. Cook at high pressure 2 minutes.

3. When cooking is complete, press Cancel or Stop and use quick release. Transfer brussels sprouts to medium bowl with slotted spoon.

4. Stir remaining 2 tablespoons orange juice into cornstarch in small bowl until smooth. Press Sauté; add honey, orange peel and cornstarch mixture to cooking liquid in pot. Cook 1 to 2 minutes or until sauce is thickened, stirring constantly.

5. Pour sauce over brussels sprouts; toss gently to coat.

Makes 4 servings

Eggplant Italiano

1 tablespoon olive oil

2 medium onions, thinly sliced

1¼ pounds eggplant, cut into 1-inch cubes

2 medium stalks celery, cut into 1-inch pieces

1 can (about 14 ounces) diced tomatoes

½ cup pitted black olives, sliced

3 tablespoons tomato sauce

2 tablespoons balsamic vinegar

1 tablespoon sugar

1 tablespoon capers, drained

1 teaspoon dried oregano or basil

¾ teaspoon salt

¼ teaspoon black pepper

1. Press Sauté; heat oil in pot. Add onions; cook and stir about 3 minutes or until softened. Add eggplant, celery, tomatoes, olives, tomato sauce, vinegar, sugar, capers, oregano, salt and pepper; mix well.

2. Secure lid and move pressure release valve to sealing or locked position. Cook at high pressure 2 minutes.

3. When cooking is complete, press Cancel or Stop and use quick release.

Makes 6 servings

Parmesan Potato Wedges

2 pounds red potatoes (about 6 medium), cut into ½-inch wedges

½ cup water

¼ cup finely chopped onion

2 tablespoons butter, cut into small pieces

1¼ teaspoons salt

1 teaspoon dried oregano

¼ teaspoon black pepper

¼ cup grated Parmesan cheese

1. Combine potatoes, water, onion, butter, salt, oregano and pepper in pot; mix well.

2. Secure lid and move pressure release valve to sealing or locked position. Cook at high pressure 3 minutes.

3. When cooking is complete, press Cancel or Stop and use quick release.

4. Transfer potatoes to serving platter; sprinkle with cheese.

Makes 4 to 6 servings

Balsamic Green Beans with Almonds

1 cup water

1 pound fresh green beans, trimmed

1 tablespoon extra virgin olive oil

2 teaspoons balsamic vinegar

½ teaspoon salt

¼ teaspoon black pepper

2 tablespoons sliced almonds, toasted*

*To toast almonds, cook and stir in small skillet over medium heat 2 to 3 minutes or until lightly browned.

1. Pour water into pot. Place rack in pot; place beans on rack. (Arrange beans perpendicular to rack to prevent beans from falling through.)

2. Secure lid and move pressure release valve to sealing or locked position. Cook at high pressure 2 minutes.

3. When cooking is complete, press Cancel or Stop and use quick release. Remove rack from pot; place beans in large bowl.

4. Add oil, vinegar, salt and pepper; toss to coat. Sprinkle with almonds just before serving.

Makes 4 servings

Fall Vegetable Medley

2 medium Yukon Gold potatoes, peeled and cut into ½-inch pieces

2 medium sweet potatoes, peeled and cut into ½-inch pieces

3 parsnips, peeled and cut into ½-inch pieces

1 bulb fennel, cut into ½-inch pieces

½ cup chopped fresh parsley

2 tablespoons butter, cut into small pieces

⅔ cup chicken or vegetable broth

2 teaspoons salt

½ teaspoon black pepper

1. Combine potatoes, sweet potatoes, parsnips, fennel, parsley and butter in pot.

2. Combine broth, salt and pepper in measuring cup or small bowl; mix well. Pour over vegetables; stir gently to coat.

3. Secure lid and move pressure release valve to sealing or locked position. Cook at high pressure 4 minutes.

4. When cooking is complete, press Cancel or Stop and use quick release.

5. Gently stir vegetables. If any liquid remains in pot, press Sauté and cook 2 to 3 minutes or until liquid has evaporated.

Makes 6 servings

Orange-Spiced Glazed Carrots

1 package (32 ounces) baby carrots

½ cup packed brown sugar

½ cup orange juice

3 tablespoons butter, cut into small pieces

¾ teaspoon ground cinnamon

½ teaspoon salt

¼ teaspoon ground nutmeg

¼ cup water

2 tablespoons cornstarch

Grated orange peel (optional)

Chopped fresh parsley (optional)

1. Combine carrots, brown sugar, orange juice, butter, cinnamon, salt and nutmeg in pot; mix well.

2. Secure lid and move pressure release valve to sealing or locked position. Cook at high pressure 2 minutes.

3. When cooking is complete, press Cancel or Stop and use quick release.

4. Stir water into cornstarch in small bowl until smooth. Press Sauté; add cornstarch mixture to carrots. Cook and stir 1 to 2 minutes or until sauce is thickened. Garnish with orange peel and parsley.

Makes 6 servings

DESSERTS

Spiced Chocolate Bread Pudding

1½ cups whipping cream

4 ounces unsweetened chocolate, coarsely chopped

2 eggs, beaten

½ cup sugar

1 teaspoon vanilla

¾ teaspoon ground cinnamon, plus additional for garnish

½ teaspoon ground allspice

⅛ teaspoon salt

3 cups cubed Hawaiian-style sweet bread, challah or brioche bread (½-inch cubes)

½ cup currants

1 cup water

Whipped cream (optional)

1. Spray 6- to 7-inch (1½-quart) soufflé dish or round baking dish that fits inside pot with nonstick cooking spray. Heat cream to a simmer in medium saucepan over medium heat. Remove from heat. Add chocolate; stir until melted and smooth.

2. Beat eggs in large bowl. Add sugar, vanilla, ¾ teaspoon cinnamon, allspice and salt; mix well. Add chocolate mixture; stir until well blended. Add bread and currants; stir gently until completely coated. Pour into prepared soufflé dish; smooth top. Cover dish tightly with foil.

3. Pour water into pot. Place rack in pot; place soufflé dish on rack.

4. Secure lid and move pressure release valve to sealing or locked position. Cook at high pressure 35 minutes.

5. When cooking is complete, use natural release for 10 minutes, then release remaining pressure.

6. Remove soufflé dish from pot. Remove foil; serve warm or at room temperature. Top with whipped cream and additional cinnamon, if desired.

Makes 6 to 8 servings

Custard Brûlée

5 egg yolks

½ cup granulated sugar

¼ teaspoon salt

1 cup whipping cream

1 cup milk

1 teaspoon vanilla

¼ teaspoon ground cinnamon

Ground nutmeg (optional)

1 cup water

¼ cup packed brown sugar

1. Whisk egg yolks, granulated sugar and salt in medium bowl until blended. Add cream, milk and vanilla; whisk until well blended. Pour into 6- to 7-inch (1½-quart) soufflé dish or round baking dish that fits inside pot. Sprinkle with cinnamon and nutmeg, if desired. Cover dish tightly with foil.

2. Pour water into pot. Place rack in pot; place soufflé dish on rack.

3. Secure lid and move pressure release valve to sealing or locked position. Cook at high pressure 35 minutes.

4. When cooking is complete, press Cancel or Stop and use quick release.

5. Remove soufflé dish from pot. Remove foil; cool to room temperature. Cover and refrigerate 3 to 4 hours or until chilled.

6. Just before serving, preheat broiler. Sprinkle brown sugar evenly over top of custard. Broil 4 inches from heat 1 to 2 minutes or until sugar bubbles and browns.

Makes 6 to 8 servings

Rich Chocolate Pudding

1½ cups whipping cream

4 ounces bittersweet chocolate, chopped

4 egg yolks

⅓ cup packed brown sugar

1 tablespoon unsweetened cocoa powder

1 teaspoon vanilla

¼ teaspoon salt

1½ cups water

1. Heat cream to a simmer in medium saucepan over medium heat. Remove from heat. Add chocolate; stir until chocolate is melted and mixture is smooth.

2. Whisk egg yolks, brown sugar, cocoa, vanilla and salt in large bowl until well blended. Gradually add hot chocolate mixture, whisking constantly until blended. Strain into 6- to 7-inch (1½-quart) soufflé dish or round baking dish that fits inside pot. Cover dish tightly with foil.

3. Pour water into pot. Place rack in pot; place soufflé dish on rack.

4. Secure lid and move pressure release valve to sealing or locked position. Cook at low pressure 22 minutes.

5. When cooking is complete, use natural release for 5 minutes, then release remaining pressure.

6. Remove soufflé dish from pot. Remove foil; cool to room temperature. Cover and refrigerate at least 3 hours or up to 2 days.

Makes 6 servings

Pumpkin Custard

3 eggs

1 can (15 ounces) solid-pack pumpkin

1 can (14 ounces) sweetened condensed milk (not evaporated milk)

1 teaspoon ground cinnamon, plus additional for garnish

1 teaspoon finely chopped candied ginger *or* ½ teaspoon ground ginger

¼ teaspoon ground cloves

⅛ teaspoon salt

1 cup water

Whipped cream (optional)

1. Whisk eggs in medium bowl. Add pumpkin, sweetened condensed milk, 1 teaspoon cinnamon, ginger, cloves and salt; whisk until well blended and smooth. Pour into 6 (6-ounce) ramekins or custard cups. Cover each ramekin tightly with foil.

2. Pour water into pot; place rack in pot. Arrange ramekins on rack, stacking as necessary.

3. Secure lid and move pressure release valve to sealing or locked position. Cook at high pressure 8 minutes.

4. When cooking is complete, use natural release.

5. Remove ramekins from pot. Remove foil; cool to room temperature. Refrigerate until chilled. Top with whipped cream and additional cinnamon, if desired.

Makes 6 servings

Quick and Easy Kheer (Indian Rice Pudding)

3 cups whole milk

⅔ cup sugar

1 cup uncooked basmati rice, rinsed and drained

½ cup golden raisins

3 whole green cardamom pods *or* ¼ teaspoon ground cardamon

¼ teaspoon salt

Grated orange peel (optional)

Pistachio nuts (optional)

1. Combine milk and sugar in pot; stir until sugar is dissolved. Add rice, raisins, cardamom and salt; mix well.

2. Secure lid and move pressure release valve to sealing or locked position. Cook at high pressure 5 minutes.

3. When cooking is complete, use natural release for 10 minutes, then release remaining pressure.

4. Stir rice pudding well before serving. (Pudding will thicken upon standing.) Garnish with orange peel and pistachios.

Makes 6 to 8 servings

Very Berry Cheesecake

CRUST

¾ cup honey graham cracker crumbs (about 5 whole crackers)

3 tablespoons butter, melted

CHEESECAKE

2 packages (8 ounces each) cream cheese, at room temperature

½ cup sugar

2 eggs, at room temperature

1 teaspoon vanilla

1 cup fresh blueberries*

2 cups water

TOPPING

½ cup seedless raspberry jam

1 cup fresh raspberries*

If blueberries or raspberries are unavailable, substitute seasonal berries or a mix of berries.

1. Cut parchment paper to fit bottom of 7½-inch springform pan that fits loosely inside pot. Lightly spray bottom and side of pan with nonstick cooking spray. Wrap bottom and side of pan with foil.

2. Combine graham cracker crumbs and melted butter in small bowl; mix well. Pat mixture onto bottom and about ½ inch up side of prepared pan. Freeze 10 minutes.

3. Meanwhile, beat cream cheese and sugar in large bowl with electric mixer at medium-high speed until light and fluffy. Add eggs, one at a time, beating well after each addition. Stir in vanilla. Sprinkle blueberries over crust in prepared pan. Pour batter over blueberries.

4. Cover pan tightly with foil. Pour water into pot. Place rack in pot; place pan on rack. Secure lid and move pressure release valve to sealing or locked position. Cook at high pressure 33 minutes.

5. When cooking is complete, press Cancel or Stop and use quick release. Remove pan from pot. Remove foil; cool 1 hour. Run thin knife around edge of cheesecake to loosen (do not remove side of pan). Refrigerate 2 to 3 hours or overnight.

6. Remove side and bottom of pan; transfer cheesecake to serving plate, if desired. Heat jam in small saucepan over low heat (or microwave in glass measuring cup), stirring until smooth. Spoon melted jam over cheesecake; top with raspberries.

Makes 6 to 8 servings

Cinnamon Raisin Bread Pudding

4 to 5 cups cubed day-old French bread (1-inch cubes)

1 cup raisins

2 cups milk

2 eggs

1 egg yolk

¼ cup granulated sugar

⅛ teaspoon ground cinnamon

⅛ teaspoon ground nutmeg

1½ cups water

Vanilla Rum Sauce (recipe follows, optional)

1. Spray 6- to 7-inch (1½-quart) soufflé dish or round baking dish that fits inside pot with nonstick cooking spray. Combine bread cubes and raisins in prepared dish; toss to distribute raisins evenly.

2. Whisk milk, eggs, egg yolk, sugar, cinnamon and nutmeg in medium bowl until well blended. Pour over bread mixture; press bread down into liquid. Cover dish tightly with foil; let stand 15 minutes.

3. Pour water into pot. Place rack in pot; place soufflé dish on rack.

4. Secure lid and move pressure release valve to sealing or locked position. Cook at high pressure 35 minutes. Meanwhile, prepare Vanilla Rum Sauce, if desired.

5. When cooking is complete, use natural release for 10 minutes, then release remaining pressure.

6. Remove soufflé dish from pot. Remove foil; serve bread pudding warm with sauce.

Makes 6 to 8 servings

Vanilla Rum Sauce: Beat 2 egg yolks and ¼ cup sugar in small bowl until light and fluffy. Heat 1 cup whipping cream to a simmer in medium saucepan over medium-high heat. Slowly add egg yolk mixture, whisking constantly 2 minutes. Remove from heat; strain into medium bowl. Stir in 2 tablespoons dark rum or brandy and ¼ teaspoon vanilla. Serve warm or at room temperature. Makes about 1¼ cups.

Chocolate Surprise Crème Brûlée

3 ounces bittersweet chocolate, finely chopped

5 egg yolks

1¾ cups whipping cream

½ cup granulated sugar

¼ teaspoon salt

1 teaspoon vanilla

1 cup water

¼ cup demerara or raw sugar

1. Spray bottoms of 5 (6-ounce) ramekins or custard cups with nonstick cooking spray. Divide chocolate evenly among ramekins.

2. Whisk egg yolks in medium bowl. Combine cream, granulated sugar and salt in medium saucepan; bring to a simmer over medium heat. Slowly pour ¼ cup hot cream mixture into egg yolks, whisking until blended. Add remaining cream mixture in thin, steady stream, whisking constantly. Pour through fine mesh strainer into clean bowl. Stir in vanilla. Ladle custard mixture into prepared ramekins over chocolate. Cover each ramekin tightly with foil.

3. Pour water into pot; place rack in pot. Arrange ramekins on rack, stacking as necessary.

4. Secure lid and move pressure release valve to sealing or locked position. Cook at high pressure 6 minutes.

5. When cooking is complete, use natural release for 10 minutes, then release remaining pressure. Remove ramekins from pot; cool to room temperature. Refrigerate until ready to serve.

6. Just before serving, preheat broiler. Place ramekins on baking sheet; sprinkle tops of custards with demerara sugar. Broil 4 inches from heat 1 to 2 minutes or until sugar bubbles and browns.

Makes 5 servings

Applesauce Custard

1½ cups unsweetened applesauce

½ teaspoon ground cinnamon

¼ teaspoon salt

4 eggs, at room temperature

½ cup half-and-half

¼ cup unsweetened apple juice concentrate

⅛ teaspoon ground nutmeg

1 cup water

1. Combine applesauce, cinnamon and salt in medium bowl; mix well. Whisk in eggs, half-and-half and apple juice concentrate until well blended. Pour into 6- to 7-inch (1½-quart) soufflé dish or round baking dish that fits inside pot. Sprinkle with nutmeg. Cover dish tightly with foil.

2. Pour water into pot. Place rack in pot; place soufflé dish on rack.

3. Secure lid and move pressure release valve to sealing or locked position. Cook at high pressure 30 minutes.

4. When cooking is complete, use natural release for 10 minutes, then release remaining pressure.

5. Remove soufflé dish from pot. Remove foil; cool to room temperature. Serve custard at room temperature or chilled.

Makes 6 servings

Chocolate Rice Pudding

1 cup water

1 cup uncooked long grain rice

½ teaspoon salt, divided

1½ cups milk

½ cup sugar

2 tablespoons cornstarch

½ teaspoon vanilla

½ cup semisweet chocolate chips

Whipped cream (optional)

Chocolate curls (optional)

1. Combine water, rice and ¼ teaspoon salt in pot; mix well.

2. Secure lid and move pressure release valve to sealing or locked position. Cook at high pressure 4 minutes.

3. When cooking is complete, use natural release for 10 minutes, then release remaining pressure.

4. Whisk milk, sugar, cornstarch, vanilla and remaining ¼ teaspoon salt in small bowl until well blended. Stir into cooked rice.

5. Press Sauté; cook and stir 5 minutes. Add chocolate chips; stir until melted and smooth. Garnish with whipped cream and chocolate curls.

Makes 6 servings

PRESSURE COOKING TIMES

Meat	MINUTES UNDER PRESSURE	PRESSURE	RELEASE
Beef, Bone-in Short Ribs	35 to 45	High	Natural
Beef, Brisket	60 to 75	High	Natural
Beef, Ground	8	High	Natural
Beef, Roast (round, rump or shoulder)	60 to 70	High	Natural
Beef, Stew Meat	20 to 25	High	Natural or Quick
Lamb, Chops	5 to 10	High	Quick
Lamb, Leg or Shanks	35 to 40	High	Natural
Lamb, Stew Meat	12 to 15	High	Quick
Pork, Baby Back Ribs	25 to 30	High	Natural
Pork, Chops	7 to 10	High	Quick
Pork, Ground	5	High	Quick
Pork, Loin	15 to 25	High	Natural
Pork, Shoulder or Butt	45 to 60	High	Natural
Pork, Stew Meat	15 to 20	High	Quick

Poultry

Poultry	MINUTES UNDER PRESSURE	PRESSURE	RELEASE
Chicken Breasts, Bone-in	7 to 10	High	Quick
Chicken Breasts, Boneless	5 to 8	High	Quick
Chicken Thigh, Bone-in	10 to 14	High	Natural
Chicken Thigh, Boneless	8 to 10	High	Natural
Chicken Wings	10 to 12	High	Quick
Chicken, Whole	22 to 26	High	Natural
Eggs, Hard-Cooked (3 to 12)	9	Low	Quick
Turkey Breast, Bone-in	25 to 30	High	Natural
Turkey Breast, Boneless	15 to 20	High	Natural
Turkey Legs	35 to 40	High	Natural
Turkey, Ground	8 to 10	High	Quick

Seafood

Seafood	MINUTES UNDER PRESSURE	PRESSURE	RELEASE
Cod	2 to 3	Low	Quick
Crab	2 to 3	Low	Quick
Halibut	6	Low	Quick
Mussels	1 to 2	Low	Quick
Salmon	4 to 5	Low	Quick
Scallops	1	Low	Quick
Shrimp	2 to 3	Low	Quick
Swordfish	4 to 5	Low	Quick
Tilapia	3	Low	Quick

Dried Beans and Legumes

	UNSOAKED	SOAKED	PRESSURE	RELEASE
Black Beans	22 to 25	8 to 10	High	Natural
Black-Eyed Peas	9 to 11	3 to 5	High	Natural
Cannellini Beans	30 to 35	8 to 10	High	Natural
Chickpeas	35 to 40	18 to 22	High	Natural
Great Northern Beans	25 to 30	7 to 10	High	Natural
Kidney Beans	20 to 25	8 to 12	High	Natural
Lentils, Brown or Green	10 to 12	n/a	High	Natural
Lentils, Red or Yellow Split	1	n/a	High	Natural
Navy Beans	20 to 25	7 to 8	High	Natural
Pinto Beans	22 to 25	8 to 10	High	Natural
Split Peas	8 to 10	n/a	High	Natural

Grains

	LIQUID PER CUP	MINUTES UNDER PRESSURE	PRESSURE	RELEASE
Barley, Pearled	2	18 to 22	High	Natural
Barley, Whole	2½	30 to 35	High	Natural
Bulgur	3	8	High	Natural
Farro	2	10 to 12	High	Natural
Grits, Medium	4	12 to 15	High	10 minute natural
Millet	1.5	1	High	Natural
Oats, Rolled	2	4 to 5	High	10 minute natural
Oats, Steel-Cut	3	10 to 13	High	10 minute natural
Quinoa	1½	1	High	10 minute natural
Polenta, Instant	3	5	High	5 minute natural
Rice, Arborio	2	6 to 7	High	Quick
Rice, Brown	1	22	High	10 minute natural
Rice, White Long Grain	1	4	High	10 minute natural

Vegetables

Vegetables	MINUTES UNDER PRESSURE	PRESSURE	RELEASE
Artichokes, Whole	9 to 12	High	Natural
Beets, Medium Whole	18 to 24	High	Quick
Brussels Sprouts, Whole	2 to 3	High	Quick
Cabbage, Sliced	3 to 5	High	Quick
Carrots, Sliced	2 to 4	High	Quick
Cauliflower, Florets	2 to 3	High	Quick
Cauliflower, Whole	3 to 5	High	Quick
Corn on the Cob	2 to 4	High	Quick
Eggplant	3 to 4	High	Quick
Fennel, Sliced	3 to 4	High	Quick
Green Beans	2 to 4	High	Quick
Kale	3	High	Quick
Leeks	3	High	Quick
Okra	3	High	Quick
Potatoes, Baby or Fingerling	6 to 10	High	Natural
Potatoes, New	7 to 9	High	Natural
Potatoes, 1-inch pieces	4 to 6	High	Quick
Potatoes, Sweet, 1-inch pieces	3	High	Quick
Potatoes, Sweet, Whole	8 to 12	High	Natural
Spinach	1	High	Quick
Squash, Acorn, Halved	7	High	Natural
Squash, Butternut, 1-inch pieces	4 to 6	High	Quick
Squash, Spaghetti, Halved	6 to 10	High	Natural
Tomatoes, cut into pieces for sauce	5	High	Natural

INDEX

METRIC CONVERSION CHART

VOLUME MEASUREMENTS (dry)

$^1/_8$ teaspoon = 0.5 mL
$^1/_4$ teaspoon = 1 mL
$^1/_2$ teaspoon = 2 mL
$^3/_4$ teaspoon = 4 mL
1 teaspoon = 5 mL
1 tablespoon = 15 mL
2 tablespoons = 30 mL
$^1/_4$ cup = 60 mL
$^1/_3$ cup = 75 mL
$^1/_2$ cup = 125 mL
$^2/_3$ cup = 150 mL
$^3/_4$ cup = 175 mL
1 cup = 250 mL
2 cups = 1 pint = 500 mL
3 cups = 750 mL
4 cups = 1 quart = 1 L

VOLUME MEASUREMENTS (fluid)

1 fluid ounce (2 tablespoons) = 30 mL
4 fluid ounces ($^1/_2$ cup) = 125 mL
8 fluid ounces (1 cup) = 250 mL
12 fluid ounces (1$^1/_2$ cups) = 375 mL
16 fluid ounces (2 cups) = 500 mL

WEIGHTS (mass)

$^1/_2$ ounce = 15 g
1 ounce = 30 g
3 ounces = 90 g
4 ounces = 120 g
8 ounces = 225 g
10 ounces = 285 g
12 ounces = 360 g
16 ounces = 1 pound = 450 g

DIMENSIONS

$^1/_{16}$ inch = 2 mm
$^1/_8$ inch = 3 mm
$^1/_4$ inch = 6 mm
$^1/_2$ inch = 1.5 cm
$^3/_4$ inch = 2 cm
1 inch = 2.5 cm

OVEN TEMPERATURES

250°F = 120°C
275°F = 140°C
300°F = 150°C
325°F = 160°C
350°F = 180°C
375°F = 190°C
400°F = 200°C
425°F = 220°C
450°F = 230°C

BAKING PAN SIZES

Utensil	Size in Inches/Quarts	Metric Volume	Size in Centimeters
Baking or Cake Pan (square or rectangular)	8×8×2	2 L	20×20×5
	9×9×2	2.5 L	23×23×5
	12×8×2	3 L	30×20×5
	13×9×2	3.5 L	33×23×5
Loaf Pan	8×4×3	1.5 L	20×10×7
	9×5×3	2 L	23×13×7
Round Layer Cake Pan	8×1½	1.2 L	20×4
	9×1½	1.5 L	23×4
Pie Plate	8×1¼	750 mL	20×3
	9×1¼	1 L	23×3
Baking Dish or Casserole	1 quart	1 L	—
	1½ quart	1.5 L	—
	2 quart	2 L	—